WHO DO YOU WANT TO BE?

8 steps to discovering your deepest desires and creating a joyful and successful life

TABLE OF CONTENTS

PREFACE

A gift to my daughters Myla and Adella,
and to you, the reader. Thanks for joining us!

I left NASA's Jet Propulsion Lab in June of 2018 to explore what life had to offer. I left what was an amazing dream job for most people, including myself, because I wanted to figure out the edges of life and see what I could create and discover. I had no idea what I was going to do but I knew I wanted to explore more and feed my curiosity about life. I accepted jobs and used every opportunity I could find to meet people I considered successful and happy. I met billionaires and mega millionaires, and many other people from all walks of life. I wanted to know what they knew about life and what I was missing. I knew that hard work alone was not going to take me where I wanted to go. I studied these people's every move, behavior and words for the short time I had with them and then studied, explored, and went after every piece of new information I could find to figure out new ways of living that bring lasting success, happiness and joy.

The events that took place during this period of my life and the ways I reacted and responded to them through my body and mind feel shocking to me still, but they revealed important truths I could no longer ignore. I went after every single one of them and figured out why things happened the way they did. The details of what happened to me are not in the scope of this book, but the lessons apply to everyone and I want to share them with my children and with you, the wonderful, curious reader who is looking for your own answers. My greatest hope is that this book answers some of your questions or leads you to discover your own answers.

In the midst of exploring life in new ways and coming across personalities, experiences and events that had something to teach me, I focused on the deep lessons each new encounter offered me. It felt like all of these people and events were showing me a map of how I needed to change and what thinking I needed to adopt so that I can create a life I truly desire. I somehow connected these seemingly unrelated events, went after every detail, studied and found the link between them. It was then that I was able to see the whole picture of how to create a life I truly desire being built in front of me, step by step, like a map I could follow. I wrote this book as a manual and a guide for myself. I must admit I wish I'd had this book when I was much younger.

I also want this book to be a gift for my two daughters. Something they can use to help them navigate their lives. An easy-to-understand and practical guide to which they can refer time and time again, when they feel lost or alone and don't know how to get back on track. Hopefully, my book will help them recognize their fire and inner power to start on the journey of becoming the best versions of themselves and living a happy and joyful life.

In school we learn how to memorize information, do complex math, and recite capitals of cities, but no class teaches us how to navigate life, how to discover who we are, or how to have what we want in life that makes us happy, feel accomplished and joyful.

On the other hand, mass media and the internet have been hypnotizing us to be ever-consuming creatures who are taught that the more we consume the happier we will be. And yet we all know that chasing shiny objects results in only temporary happiness.

There is nothing wrong with enjoying material things like a beautiful house, fancy cars, amazing vacation destinations and designer clothing. After all, we are human and life is meant to be fun, rewarding and enjoyable, and relishing the luxuries of life is natural, if that's what we want. But most of us also realize that when we sell our souls, betray ourselves and manipulate others to gain material success, we will never be happy and feel good about ourselves deep down. This is one of my most simple and valuable observations. I have closely observed many seemingly successful people who are broken, deeply depressed and alone inside.

In this small book, I share the research I have done by reading many books, both old and new, on success, happiness, and human behavior. I have also studied unique and interesting personalities and the lessons I learned are included in this book. I have always been a very curious person—always looking for answers. As an engineer, I look at seemingly unrelated events and circumstances and am able to connect the dots in ways that may not be so obvious to others. My hope is that you find this book valuable in your quest to create your most fulfilling life!

This book was also inspired by my deep reflections about some very specific events in my life. I wanted answers about why things are the way they are. I did my best to reflect on every detail of my past experiences and to figure things out. The reflection process took about eight months of meticulous work, which started with meditating at least two hours a day to prepare, organize and free my mind from distractions, and also included reading, studying, and watching countless videos—so I could concentrate on every seemingly unrelated event in my life and connect the dots.

I wanted to organize my discoveries into a book so that I, my children and anyone interested in living a joyful life could have it at their fingertips.

The format of this book is minimalist, so there is no superfluous content, but instead I have focused on ease of reading, designed to bring ultimate joy to the reader. I hope you enjoy it!

As we live our lives, we become heavier and heavier... and I do not refer to body weight but to our emotions, the behaviors and the thoughts we pick up from our parents, our environment, our schools, friends, bosses, coworkers and every other aspect of our culture. We become loaded down with so many ideas about what is right and what is wrong, and over time, all these affect our ability to feel light, cheerful and vibrant. We lose our ability to feel happy and flexible, as all children do. This book, first and foremost, aims to help you recognize and become aware of these layers of heaviness and the weight you carry and then helps you remove them one by one to feel younger, happier and bring back the child-like joy to your life.

Once you feel lighter and more joyous, then I'll show you how to create the space and the environment to live a life you truly desire. Life is short, precious and a gift. One day we wake up and realize that we no longer have time to do what we'd always wanted to do. That's the reason I wrote this book. I wanted to discover the best ways to create a life that is enjoyable, original and successful, so that I can craft an amazing life for myself and share the "how tos" with my daughters and you, my curious and lovely reader. After all, isn't that why you picked up this book? You are looking for ways to improve your life and become who you really want to be.

I promise you that this book will not disappoint you. I will share with you the essence of my research, personal experiences and paths that I found useful in creating a truly joyful life. I am excited for you to read, reflect and use the information I provide. The book is bold, direct and to the point, and may challenge some of your conventional beliefs and ways of doing things but I can assure you that you will pick up valuable insights on how to live your life the way you want to live it.

We are the only creatures on this planet with a creative mind, an intellect, and the power of imagination so that we can create our own environment. No other creature can do this.

- Bob Proctor

Life is simpler and more beautiful than we have been told. The secret to living a truly joyful life, though, is to unlearn most of what we learned at school, and what we have picked up from our immediate family and from society. Joyful experiences are within reach of every single one of us and we can create a beautiful, meaningful and blissful life if we choose to do so.

Happiness happens when you feel you are on the right path and growing; when your personal life and your professional life are balanced and when you experience growth. But here's the thing: if our happiness is bound to our personal life experiences and our profession, the minute either of these goes sideways, we feel unhappy and stressed out. The real secret of happiness is inner peace, which comes from the alignment of different aspects of life. Alignment and harmony with what your heart and soul want, what brings you deep joy, what makes you tick, feel alive and passionate.

Join me while I share with you what the different aspects of life are and how to detox, organize and energize each aspect of your life and align them to create the fulfilling life you truly deserve.

With Love,
Alina

PART 1

DISCOVER WHAT YOU TRULY WANT

STEP 1

FIGURE OUT WHAT KIND OF LIFE YOU WANT TO LIVE

BUILD AN INSPIRING VISION IN ALL AREAS OF YOUR LIFE

A good life is a combination of many aspects of your life. True happiness comes with knowing deep down who you want to be and when all areas of your life are in alignment and harmony with your grand vision, followed by a sense of growth and progress toward your unique destination. But in order to know where you want to go, you need to know what you are truly passionate about and what your deepest desires are. So what do you want? This is the question!

What is your passion?

You and I are amazing creatures. We have the power to process thoughts, apply logic, imagine things out of thin air and create ideas in our minds, feel deep emotions and create and follow a purpose in life. We are creative beings; we have the power to make decisions and steer our lives toward any destination we choose.

As we grow up, go through years of schooling, embrace the culture we live in - whether consciously or through habit - we begin to forget our true desires and instead adopt what society and our environment downloads into us, and we're rewarded with what is deemed to be a good life. The truth is that we cannot be truly happy unless we go back to the things we liked the most when we were seven or fourteen years old. These are the ages when most of us experience or understand what truly makes us happy before society takes its toll on us. Was it being in nature, swimming and playing in water all day, reading books or doing science projects, playing music, or doing something even more unique? What type of activity made you lose track of time? Or did you enjoy it so much, you could have done it all day long? These are clues as to who you really are and what makes you truly happy, and until you reinstate those things in your life, and design your life in a way that your days lighten your heart, you won't feel fulfilled and joyful.

Exercise

How to Remember Your Deep Desires

In our hearts, we all know our deepest desires. You might think you have forgotten about them but they are still there, deep inside you, and you can access them and revitalize them!

Find a quiet time and a relaxing place where you can be alone, put on some relaxing music, wear comfortable clothing, take an Epsom salt bath or do whatever calms you and relaxes you, then sit with a piece of paper and pen and write down the answers to the following questions:

- What makes me happy?
- What were the moments in my life when I felt most relaxed and joyful?
- What did I enjoy doing when I was 7? What about when I was around 14? Try to recall memories of moments you enjoyed the most and that felt amazing.
- What makes me feel really good about myself when I am not trying to impress anyone?
- What makes me feel intense inner joy?

Do this activity as many times as it takes to get to the answers. You will notice patterns and it will become clearer to you what brings you pure joy.

Notes

What do you do if you are not sure what your passion is?

Some people know very clearly what they like to do, what their passions are and what they want their profession to be. They may also know where they want to live and who they want to be. But many others, including myself, need to figure it out along the way. For most of us, the way to find our passion is through trial and error. Try different activities or endeavors and pay attention to how you feel when engaged in them. What part of your job do you enjoy and lose track of time doing, and what part of it do you dread? Paying attention to these experiences will give you clues to what you like to do and where your passion lies.

For many of us, our passion is not necessarily one thing that we should do for our entire life, but can be multiple things we enjoy and that we develop over time through practice. As I said above, finding your passion can be a process of trial and error. Choose something in which you have some initial interest, keep yourself engaged in it until the learning curve has passed and see how you are enjoying it over time. Do you enjoy the entire activity; can you see yourself doing it for a long period of time, maybe even for years?

For many, passion can also come from combining skills at which they are good but not necessarily great.

It is important to realize that for the majority of us, finding our passion is a process. The process begins with taking action, trying many things, learning skills that appeal to us and then figuring out a way to package, utilize and combine those skills as we develop them over time.

As you are figuring out what your passions are, you need to find ways to incorporate them into different areas of your life and create room for them to grow and enrich your life. Figuring out activities, purposes, places and things you truly enjoy is the first step toward creating a life you truly want. After all, not knowing what we want makes us a product of our environment, which forces us to live a random, *unpurposeful* and reactive life.

Our passions will change over time and we will be interested in new things, new learnings, and new adventures and these new chapters are something we should celebrate and welcome in our life as a sign of growth and progress.

Exercise

For the next three weeks, make a list of things that you do on a daily basis. Then make another list of things that make you happy. Compare the lists and adjust your life accordingly to include more of what you love to do and less of what you don't like.

Notes

STEP 2

KNOW HOW YOUR MIND WORKS & WHAT YOUR BODY NEEDS

The second step on the journey to living a happy life is to know your mind and body and how it functions. We humans have almost unlimited potential within us. Everything we need to create joy, happiness, success, riches, fulfillment and deep satisfaction is already within us. It amazes me even now that our school system fails to teach us about our inner powers and our internal mechanism of creating power for ourselves. Let's explore this very important subject now and familiarize ourselves with the unbelievable innate powers we have within. Let's get to it!

Mind and body are deeply connected and it's hard to talk about one without the other. We used to talk about mind and body separately but today we know that they are deeply intertwined and that they either work together or against each other.

Your mind is a collection of thoughts and memories and it directly affects your body in both positive and negative ways, depending on your thought processes. On the other hand, how you treat your body affects your mind, including what you eat, how you restore, your habits, how you move and how you take care of your body. All this is connected to your mind.

How does our mind function?

Our minds consist of two parts - the conscious and the subconscious. About 95% of our actions are controlled by the subconscious mind, which is not only in our brain but also in our nervous system. The subconscious mind is the habit mind, and the automatic part of the brain and body that does its job without having to think about it. For example, your body knows by default how to breathe and your heart knows how to beat and so on. While the conscious mind has the ability to choose, the subconscious mind does not and therefore works like a machine that does what it is told to do.

Only about 5% of our actions are controlled by the conscious mind. The conscious mind is the thinking mind, or the analytical mind, and it is what differentiates us from other animals.

When we are born and until the age of 7, we are mostly controlled by the subconscious mind, which acts like a sponge—absorbing everything we see, hear and feel from the environment and forming our personality, our habits, and our belief system.

The subconscious mind that you have as an adult is the result of the programming you experienced in early childhood and the environment to which you have been exposed throughout your life. In addition to our external environment, let's not forget the genes that were passed to us from our parents and grandparents. These are also part of our subconscious mind, which works much like the operating system of a computer. All other programs, such as your skills, what you do and don't do well, how you behave, talk, eat, think about yourself and others, and most everything else work within that operating system. These characteristics are like little apps operating within the main operating system of your subconscious mind.

And here is a super important concept about the subconscious mind. If you are blocked in some areas of your life - no matter how hard you try or how many times you start over, it is probably due to limitations and errors in your subconscious programming that you may not be aware of. To truly improve our lives in some or even all areas, we need to upgrade our programming, aka our operating system.

Let's say you are trying to improve your financial life and make more money. You work hard, do your best and are committed but you may feel that no matter what you do or how hard you work, you are unable to achieve the level of financial success you seek. When you feel stuck in such a situation, there is likely one or more limiting beliefs and old programming in your subconscious mind that is working against the goal you have set for yourself, and until you upgrade and change your programming, you will repeat the same blockage, circumstance and bad luck over and over again.

The most encouraging news is that we can absolutely change this old programming. In fact, it is our responsibility to upgrade ourselves in order to be able to live the life we truly want and to help our families, friends or anyone else with whom we are socially engaged. As humans, it is our obligation to show up as our best selves for our families' sake and for society, because if we don't, the people we love the most and society as a whole will be damaged. You might ask why this is. The reason is that when we engage with the world with our wounded, error-prone self, we project our shortcomings and the unhealed negative emotions of our past experiences onto others and we might accidentally hurt, damage or misconduct others.

Neuroplasticity is the scientific name for our ability to change the wiring and the physical shape of our brain... even many years beyond our childhood and throughout our entire life. This is huge; it means that we are no longer the product of our environment but are instead the creators of our own lives. We can no longer blame our environment or childhood but have the opportunity to accept where we are in life, figure out what we want moving forward and then begin the process - explained in this book - to create the life we want!

When you take charge of your own life, and consciously decide and choose what kind of life you want, you begin to change your brain and your mind. You start behaving like that new person you desire to become and when you do that, you start finding opportunities and attracting ways that will take you to your destination. You **DECIDE** what you want, using your conscious mind and then give the job of **HOW** to get there to your subconscious mind, which is designed for this task and which will work day and night to find ways for you to achieve your goals. Your subconscious mind is a goal-seeking device, and once you set your goal using methods explained here, it will look for ways for you to accomplish it. This will become almost an effortless way to realizing the vision you create for yourself. This is the map I have observed many successful people use to create a better life for themselves.

Mind and body connection

Our minds are made up of thoughts and memories. They are designed to think. This is why quieting the mind does not really work. Together our mind and body work like a machine that functions automatically based on programming - or the subconscious mind that runs the show. So if our minds are made up of thoughts, it's probably a good idea that we know what thoughts are and where they come from. Thoughts are words and images from memories, and are triggered by a present event or habit, new experiences, and new learnings.

When a thought arises, if we pay attention to it, it will cause electrochemical reactions in the brain and will release neurotransmitters that generate feelings and sensations in the body that affect different parts, such as the heart, lungs, stomach, posture and so forth. Feelings are what make us act in certain ways. We act based on feelings no matter how rational we believe we are!

Exercise

Build Awareness of How Your Thoughts Change Your Body

Next time you have a thought, try to be aware of how it changes your breathing, the sensations in your neck and shoulders, and in your stomach.

When you have good thoughts, you might feel warmth in your stomach, your breathing is deep and your shoulders are relaxed, but when you have bad thoughts, you feel tense, your breathing is shallow, and your muscles tighten.

This illustrates how what you think changes your body and makes you act in certain ways. If you think predominantly good thoughts, your body will change in certain ways and so will your actions, thereby creating positive results in your life.

Notes

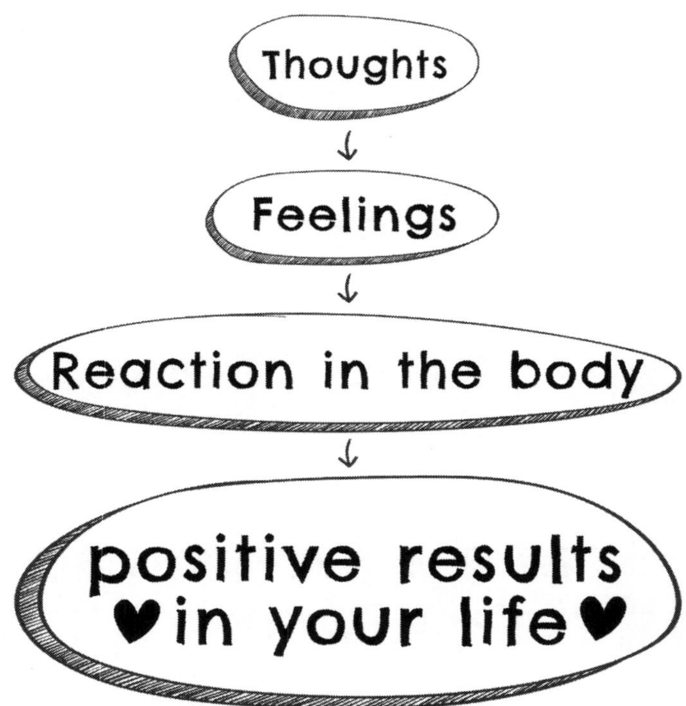

Actions and reactions are what you do, what you attract and how you respond to your environment. Good thoughts make you feel positive emotions, which cause you to take good actions and good actions, in turn, generate positive results in life. In other words, everything starts from within you, so nothing *out there* will bring you lasting joy and happiness. Nothing! You create happiness or misery in your life through your own thought processes. Think good thoughts; create good results. Think negative thoughts; create negative results. I'll say it again — nothing outside of you can provide lasting happiness. This does not mean that striving to improve our financial position or enjoying material things is wrong. We're all entitled to want to live in a nice home, drive an expensive car, travel to exotic places, and most importantly, to not have to worry about money, and we should all strive to enjoy a full life.

Most of us have been taught that in order to feel happy and good, we need an external stimulator, but that is a temporary fix. The stimulator's effect goes away rather quickly and it never gives us the lasting joy we are looking for. So don't wait for an outside trigger to be happy, motivated, engaged with life and fulfilled. Create it for yourself.

If you want to predict your future, pay attention to what you think, because what you think about most is what you focus on and what you pay attention to will expand and will shape your reality.

This is important because it means that what you think affects how you feel, and how you feel determines what your body does and what actions you take. The actions you take determine your outcome in life. So to change your life, think good thoughts.

The key to changing your life for the better through good thoughts is believing these positive and hopeful thoughts, so that they can generate the right feelings and those feelings will generate your actions and ultimately your results. This is what I mean when I say we are the co-creators of our lives. The other co-creators are things outside of us over which we don't have much control. Where you were born, what family you were born into, how others behave and how the universe functions are all out of our control. The best bet we can make is focusing on what we can control, which are our thoughts and our internal world. When mastered, this can be used to create a beautiful life. We all have two choices; act like a victim, and live life as the helpless creatures we were born as, or take responsibility for our own life and turn it into a masterpiece. The choice is ours!

Our main goal every single day should be having good, productive thoughts. That's why we meditate - to have more awareness of our thoughts and to be able to control and direct our thinking. Meditation allows us to build awareness of our thoughts and their patterns and see how thoughts that randomly pop up can be noticed but not engaged with, much like when you watch clouds pass by overhead. Eventually, you're able to ignore the negative thoughts and accept and "generate" better ones. Yes, you can and should generate positive thoughts instead of relying on the automatic ones that pop up randomly.

To generate more positive thoughts, though, we need to create an environment for positivity. We should associate with positive people and seek out good vibes, and pay attention to the design of our space and our environment, because these things also influence our thinking. That's why successful people invest in positive and novel experiences, books and learning, good friends and beauty—because these things keep us on the right track and promote positive thinking, which is key to building happiness.

If you pay attention to your thoughts, you might notice at first that you have many negative thoughts during the day. These are generated by the subconscious, which simply repeats old, familiar behavior. It is merely a program whose job is to generate negative thoughts to keep you in familiar and known environments to protect you from danger and the unknown. This is simply how our brain works. It is wired to protect us from danger and the best way it knows how to do that is to scare/steer us away from the unknown. This is precisely why change is hard. Our subconscious mind runs on a familiar program and wants to keep us from moving to unknown territory.

THINKING

Let's explore more about thoughts, since they are such an important stepping stone in our path toward happiness. Since thoughts become ideas and ideas become feelings and feelings create our internal vibe and determine our actions, and our actions and vibes become real things and create results, we should never allow this cycle to work backwards; in other words, allow the physical world around us to define or affect our thinking. This is what taking responsibility for our own lives means. Nothing that happens outside of us and outside of our control should affect us negatively. I know this is super hard, but it's achievable with practice and patience. If we allow everything that happens externally to affect us and move us in different directions, we are never going to plant the seeds of happiness, joy and success and see them flourish, because the wind will blow and take our seeds away from us.

This brings me to a point I want to make - jealousy and envy of other people's accomplishments is foolish.

People who accomplish things in life first decide and develop their accomplishments in their minds—in other words, they build a picture in their imagination of what they want to accomplish, and then develop ideas and take specific actions to manifest these accomplishments. They take care of the seeds they plant, so being envious is pointless, because we are all given the same tools, the same power of mind and the same universal law applies to everyone. Our paths, our destinations and our true wants might be different, but we have all been given the power of choice and the power of imagination.

Do you want to know a little secret? Your subconscious mind - what controls your body - does not know the difference between reality and imagination. So think good thoughts and imagine what you want, and feel the emotions of your good-vibe imagination, because imagination is an incredibly powerful tool that makes things a reality if repeated enough times.

Thoughts are things. Whenever you think with emotion, your body accepts it and thinks it is real.

Be nice to yourself

Most of us say things to ourselves that we would never say to others. What we tell ourselves is a lot more important than what others tell us. Say nice things to yourself. Your thinking controls everything! You become what you think.

> Think good thoughts. Choose thoughts that serve you and your future.

Humans operate in three ways: intellectual, emotional and physical. Once you make a decision with your intellectual mind (thinking and deciding), you become emotionally involved with it. Your emotional state dictates your physical actions and your actions determine what you attract in your life. Therefore, think about what you want with positive emotion and you will already have it.

There is a gestation period before you are able to see what you want in the physical world. Once your subconscious mind, which controls your body, is in agreement with your goal, it will find the right actions to take—day and night seeking the goal that it has been assigned—and will eventually take you to the destination you imagined and desired.

No one can make you think about what you don't want to think about. Ideas, words and images come to you all the time and from all directions, trying to change what you think, but the final choice is yours. You choose to decide what you think and what you think is crucial because your body is an instrument of the mind, so when you think a thought with emotions involved, your body has no other choice but to act on it. Think a good thought, and your body will act positively, will have more energy, and will be more creative, happy and healthy. Think negative thoughts and your body will be anxious, nervous, tired, get sick, have disease (dis-ease = a body that is not in ease) and have low energy vibration. The choice is yours. So choose your thoughts wisely.

When you choose to think a negative thought, you build a negative idea in your mind and when you attach emotions to that thought, you embed that idea into your subconscious, which does not have the ability to choose. When an idea is given to the subconscious mind, your body has to react to it—it does not have any other choice.

Until you change your thinking, you will always recycle your experience.

Action Items:

Come up with three deep desires. Make sure they are not intermediary goals, or goals that you **think** you need to achieve in order to accomplish the goals that will give you lasting joy, happiness and success. Your path to joy, happiness and success might be different from what you think it is. It's important to leave the path to your innermost desire to your subconscious, because this part of your mind is more adept at finding the fastest and shortest path, and use your intelligent mind to decide what it is you really want to achieve.

For instance, for me, one of my innermost goals since I was about nine years old has been to be a writer. But what kind of books to write and how to write them is an intermediary goal that I let my subconscious mind figure out.

The ideas and the insights will come to you suddenly and subtly. Pay attention to them, take a quick note before you forget them and then take action on them as soon as possible. These ideas are your intuition, since you already assigned the 'How' to your subconscious mind.

Notes

Universal laws you haven't been taught at school

The idea you develop in your mind is the spiritual seed you implant. You need to take care of it by providing an environment where it can grow! Just like when you plant a seed, you water it, make sure it has soil and sunshine and is in an environment that will support its growth. You patiently wait while you take care of it and then one day it sprouts.

This universe we live in operates on laws. We know that nights are followed by mornings. We know that spring comes after winter. We know that when you let go of an object inside the earth's atmosphere, it will always travel down, not up. These are the laws of the universe and the more we are aware of them and operate in harmony with them, the more enjoyable our lives will be and the more likely we'll be to create a life we truly want.

It's simple - we can use the power of universal laws to work in our favor to manifest more of what we want in life. Much like the way the earth operates, when you plant the seed of an idea in your mind (the soil), the root grows first. This is your inner growth and it never comes from outside but always from inside! That's a universal law. We must plant the seed inside of ourselves first, and let it grow roots. If we take care of the seed, and provide the environment for it to grow—internally and externally, one day we will see it sprout!

Do not allow external forces to destroy your seed. Therefore, do not share it or talk about it with people who don't have the same desire or beliefs as you do. They will kill it in a second. Let the seed take root inside of you by getting involved with it emotionally, because your body operates on emotions. Your nervous system works on emotions. Water it with positive, hopeful and powerful emotions. STEP 6 - "Get Out of Your Own Way" offers many methods to help you grow and water your idea, and will help make sure that you don't accidently kill it.

Realize that you have choices in life. Don't act like a victim. If you really want to change your life, you can do so at any time. Life is full of choices! And you are empowered! So put yourself first. And remember that this is not a selfish act but is your responsibility to grow, flourish and become a better version of yourself, as long as you don't discriminate, abuse, bother or unfairly treat other human beings. Our personal growth is a gift to others because the best way to help others is to first help ourselves so that we can contribute to the growth of those around us and be able to inspire and help them.

You are capable of anything. Anything you want to do or be! This is true for both good and bad goals. Your mind does not really care what you plant in there. You can grow beautiful flowers or poisons in the soil of your mind. The choice is yours, as long as you can imagine yourself being that person. This power of the mind can be used to bring good to you and others or it can turn you into a beast who causes suffering for yourself and others. So plant good seeds and harvest good results that will lift your soul. Truly believing is the key, and by that I mean it should come from your true desire—not what others want you to be or how others measure success, happiness and a good life. It needs to be your deep and true vision and no one else's.

Summary

The goal of STEP 2 was to help you become familiar with how your brain and your mind function and how they affect your body, your actions and your results. The take-away of STEP 2 is that our continuous negative thoughts make us feel heavy, run-down and old. So we absolutely must get rid of them! This will be covered in greater detail in STEP 6 - "Get Out of Your Own Way."

Exercise

Let Go of Negative Thoughts

- Set aside 10 minutes of quiet time and listen to the negative dialogue in your mind: I can't, I won't be able to, I don't have the talent, the time, etc. Let it all out! Too old, too young, what's the point, etc. Empty out all of these negative thoughts and excuses.
- Let it all out, breathe deeply and let it go.
- Replace the negativity with positive thoughts.
- Every negative statement, feeling or thought should be replaced with a positive one.
- A negative thought such as "I am not good enough" should be changed and followed by "I soon will be good enough. I am learning and making progress every day."
- What's left will be something wonderful.

Notes

STEP 3

DESIGN YOUR ENVIRONMENT

Now that we know what the grand vision of our life is and we are familiar with how our mind works and how we can utilize it to create a fantastic life for ourselves, it is time to discuss the different areas of our lives. Each area needs to support the big vision and they all need to be in alignment with each other so that we can build the foundation of our dream lives in this environment and plant the seed of happiness in it.

DESIGN YOUR ATTITUDE - THE MOST IMPORTANT FACTOR OF SUCCESS

Ever wondered why so few people become successful and joyous in life and so many do not? Why so many people struggle with money, their health, and relationships, while fewer live a happy, prosperous and joyful life? The real secret to live a truly joyous life is attitude. But what is attitude? If it is such an important factor in our happiness level, can we cultivate and change it?

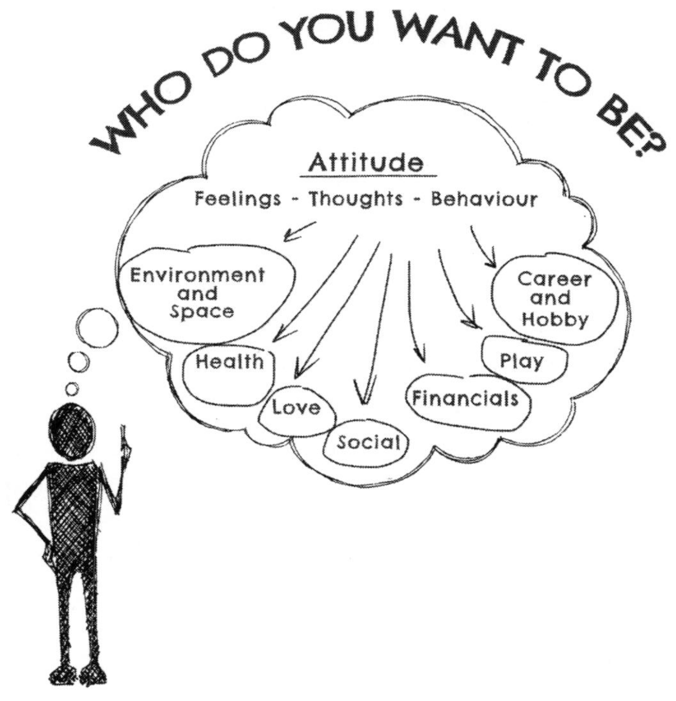

Attitude is a combination of your mood, how you think, how you feel and how you act. In other words, as we live in the world, we are exposed to external factors, such as how others behave, what they do to us, the weather, and so many other things that are out of our control. How we behave, respond and communicate with the environment around us and how we take responsibility for what we *can* control (our own thoughts and our behavior) are the most important factors in determining the level of success, happiness, and joy we experience in life.

External events are just that, "external," meaning we don't have much control over them. As a matter of fact, nothing that happens out there is bad or good, it just is. But we can control how we think, interpret and react to external events. Ever notice how positive, happy people with a good attitude seem like magnets for success? Everyone wants to work with them and associate with them. These are the people who are generally called lucky.

> When we start on a journey to design and create the life we truly want, we must start with who we want to be - our attitude and our personality.

It's time to reveal another secret: we can actually design and cultivate a positive attitude. We can design and work toward changing our attitudes and our personality and cultivate joy and success. When we do this, we become a magnet that attracts good luck, opportunities, success and joy. As I studied successful, happy and joyful people, I realized that they are positive in general. They do not allow external events to destroy their inner peace or cause them to overreact to situations. These people have an 'attitude of gratitude.' They are appreciative of their lives, their opportunities and they enjoy what they have. They are helpful, good-hearted and generous people. On the other hand, they have clear boundaries in their lives. Since they already know what they want in life, they say no to anything that does not serve them and will distract them from their own goals and dreams. And they say yes to opportunities and new experiences that align with their deepest desires.

Exercise

Who Do You Want To Be?

- Find a quiet place and sit down with a piece of paper and decide what kind of attitude you want to have. One that will support your grand vision in life.
- Who do you want to be?
- How do you want to behave around family, friends, co-workers, business associates, or anyone else?
- How do you want to be remembered?
- Who do you want to be when no one is watching you?
- What empowering truths do you know about yourself?
- What are your non-negotiable values that no matter what, you won't compromise on?
- What are the attributes and qualities you want to install in yourself?
- What do you want to value in life? Friends, family, good deeds, something else?

Notes

The point is that it is a conscious choice to "decide" who you want to be. We are not stuck with what we have been given. We have the power to design our lives. Once you know exactly who you want to be, you are halfway there. The rest of it comes from staying consistent and coming up with ways to close the gap between who you are now and who you want to become. Congrats on figuring out the first half!

> Every morning, when you wake up, the first question you should ask yourself is: Who do I want to be today?

Design your environment for your ideal seed to grow

What kind of environment do you want to live in? What kind of a home do you want to have? What are the colors, how many rooms and what are their shapes? What kind of furniture and objects are in each room? Is your kitchen retro or modern? Is your bathtub a clawfoot or jetted to be a whirlpool? Do you have floor to ceiling bookshelves, plants everywhere, photos on the walls?

Start building a vision board, either in a notebook or on your computer, and add pictures of the spaces you would like to live in. All of this together is your vision board, which will continually remind you what kind of space you want to live in. Your subconscious will take note and will automatically guide you to make the right decisions to get you closer to your vision and mission. Vision boards are one of the most valuable tools you can use to achieve the life you want. More on the vision board in Step 4 - "Make It All Happen Like Magic."

Now that you know what you want your future space to look like, your current environment should support your vision and be a simpler and smaller version of your desired space. Your current environment, no matter where it is, how big or how far away it is from your vision needs to support your ideal and desired space. Surround yourself with clean, organized, inspiring and lovely things.

Everything around you influences your subconscious mind. Remember, one way to influence the subconscious is through repetition, so when you're in the same environment every day for years, the objects and the vibe of the environment influence our subconscious mind without us knowing. Therefore, to positively influence our subconscious mind through our repeating environments - aka our living spaces - the objects, the designs and the vibe in each room should reflect the purpose and focus of that room. For example, your bedroom should have more romantic images and a calming and relaxing vibe as opposed to business books and success-related items. Your workspace, on the other hand, should not have many pictures of family, vacations and social life because that space is where you should be able to focus on business.

Clutter

Clutter in the house usually means that some areas of your mind are cluttered. Clear the space and watch how it calms your mind. Clutter blocks your creativity, makes your mind busy with unnecessary thoughts and steals away calmness and positivity. This clutter is simply the external, easy-to-see manifestation of how we've become cluttered in other areas of our lives.

When we're blocked by too much *stuff,* we get stuck. Too many objects from the past keep you in the past and prevent you from imagining and making room for the future you want to create. Ideas and visions remain wishful and theoretical. We can't see a clear path to what we want. We may not even be able to clearly define what we want, let alone be able to go after it. Decluttering—cleaning up our act physically, mentally, and emotionally—frees us from those stuck places and helps us become proactive.

So declutter your current life and make room for your new life to take root. Remember that when you plant the seeds of your desired life, you need to take care of the seed in an environment that can help it take root and grow.

Anything you haven't used for a while that has piled up, such as old clothing, papers, objects and other unnecessary stuff keeps you in the past and keeps your mind cluttered. Remove them from your space and watch magic happen to your mood!

Design for your five senses

Once the clutter is gone, implement versions of your desired space in your current space. What you see, hear, smell, touch and taste every day affects your mood, your energy and your motivation level. Make sure the items that you see and touch bring positivity and hopefulness. Hang up quotes and paintings and decorative items that match your vision board.

Design with colors

Start using colors in your environment that speak to your soul. What colors do you want to see every day? Add pillows, flowers, and wall decor in those colors.

Design with scent

Scent is another aspect of our environment that directly affects our mood. Find essential oils and flowers that motivate you, keep your energy high and calm your mind. Design your scent space!

Design with music

Find and play music that speaks to your heart, and boosts your mood, positivity and motivation. You might find it energizing to play music when exercising, reading, working or studying. The sound of water is a natural tranquilizer, so use water fountains or other water features to block out traffic noise and other white noise in your environment.

Declutter from news/media

Working at tech companies for many years, I know first-hand how much work and expertise goes into designing products that hook you and hijack your time and attention. Many tech companies that design consumer-facing apps have full-time psychologists and human behavior designers who work day and night to instill habits in users to get them addicted to their product. Be aware of this and don't become prey for greedy corporations whose purpose is to distract you from your true self so that they can make a profit.

In terms of social media, unfollow people who make you feel bad. Don't allow the toxicity of social media to program you! Instead, make your newsfeed a place that can catalyze your growth, instead of lessen your self worth.

Design for taste

Our taste is one of the senses with which we experience life and the food we consume nourishes our bodies and gives us the energy and nutrition we need for a good life. So declutter your refrigerator and food cabinets. Remove items that are unhealthy, loaded with sugar and preservatives and ingredients that you don't even recognize, and replace them with vibrantly colored vegetables and fruits and healthy whole foods that are minimally processed and are natural. Begin to see food as fuel that supports your dreams and provides nutrition for your body. Experiencing a happy, positive and well-designed environment that touches all five senses will make you happier, more positive and more receptive to your goals.

Pro Tip

Go cold turkey and declutter every area of your life at once, taking no longer than three days to do so. This is beneficial because in just three days you will end up with a beautiful environment that you can enjoy. You will have healthy food to eat that supports your vision for your future self before negativity, overthinking, doubt and procrastination can take over. Do it and watch magic happen in your life!

Health

Having a healthy body and calm, quiet and positive mind are your most important assets in life. Without these, basic everyday life becomes a challenge that drains your life's energy and vitality.

A wise person makes their physical health and mind's wellbeing a top priority. A happy body is a body that feels light, has lots of energy and is relaxed and at ease. On the contrary, a body that has disease consumes all your energy and is demotivating. After all, our body is what we live in, and sensible people take care of their home.

While we all know that we need to take care of our body, most of us don't do it in a consistent way that provides long-term and lasting benefits. Crash diets and occasional exercising will not give you the energy level and the hormonal and chemical boosts your body needs to create the life of your dreams. What kind of a life do you want? Who do you want to be? How do you want your body to feel and what do you want it to look like?

Once you build the vision of who you want to become, then your body has a goal, and the vision and the passion for achieving the desired better version of yourself will drive you to take action.

If you have a vision of how much you want to weigh and how you want to look and feel and are still not taking action, it could be the result of one of the underlying causes that I explain below. Identifying the root cause of lack of motivation and lack of consistency is the first step toward reaching your goals. Let's take a look at these things that may be holding you back:

1. Limiting beliefs that block your action. You have thoughts like *I cannot do it*, *I will fail*, *I am not worth it*, *if I change myself, the people in my life will not like the new me*, and so on. In Step 6, you will find tips on how to discover what your limiting beliefs are and how to tackle them.
2. Your subconscious mind is not in agreement with what you are consciously trying to achieve, because your subconscious mind has a different goal. If you keep failing at something, figure out if the goal you are trying to reach is what you truly want or if it is what *others* want you to do or become.

3. Lack of habit in living a healthy life. The reasons for not having a consistently healthy lifestyle come from our family habits, our environments or our own habits. Consciously building healthy habits and designing a supportive environment is the way to change this forever. Again, refer to Step 6 for tips on building lasting habits.

4. Lack of motivation. So many of us feel that we are not motivated enough to take action. We logically know that we must take care of our bodies and live a healthy life. Most of us become motivated for a limited time, but that wears off quickly. The trick to keeping the motivation high is repeatedly reminding yourself of your vision for your body by looking at motivating pictures and wise words, and by watching and listening to motivational talks, podcasts, videos and books on a daily basis. Motivation is a daily practice and it is our job to keep ourselves motivated. Just as we can't brush our teeth once and expect our teeth to be clean for days, motivating ourselves has to take place on a daily basis if we want it to be effective.

5. Feeling overwhelmed with negative thoughts and emotions. According to research conducted by the National Science Foundation, about

70% of our thoughts are negative. This is a surprisingly high number that stops us from taking action and doing things that we know will benefit us. We allow negative thoughts and circumstances to derail our actions instead of consciously acting to live a healthier life. Step 6 will provide tips on how to keep these blockers from taking over our lives and making us reactive instead of being the creator we were born to be.

Love

Humans are love bugs. We were born to give and receive love. The emotion of love encompasses feelings of freedom, lightness, connection, care and joy, all of which are chemical reactions that take place in our brains and bodies. These feelings are transmitted throughout our entire body, to every single muscle and throughout our nervous system.

Love is the gateway to abundance, and not forgiving negative experiences of the past is a blocker of love. Most blocked energy can be released through forgiveness. When you forgive yourself for any perceived wrongdoing or wrong thinking, you will expand your life and the flow of good energy will begin. Things open up in every area, whether romance, health, physical well-being, or finances. So ask yourself, "Where in my life am I still holding on to a grudge against myself or another person?"

Forgiveness is when you can remember a past experience but no longer feel a negative charge in your body, or when you see someone who wronged you, but no longer react to or feel bad about them. Of course, forgiving someone does not mean that you should maintain a relationship with someone who hurt you. You should do your best to associate primarily with positive, joyful people and become so positive inside that the negativity of others will not affect you. Forgiveness is for you, so that you can free yourself from hurt and suffering and feel lighter and happier.

Throughout this book, I will refer to the power of forgiveness time and again and I will share practices to help you forgive and let go of the past so that you can fly in freedom and experience joy that you didn't know was possible.

Give love and receive love

It's a time-honored axiom because it's true: In order to love others, we must first love ourselves. In fact, self-love must overflow so you have plenty to give to others. Loving yourself is not a selfish act because you cannot love anyone else if you don't first love yourself.

If you truly love yourself, you cannot hate the experiences that shaped you. They made you the wise person you are today.

Give the best of you to your relationships and expect the best back. Great relationships, like anything in life, require attention and work. They are the result of mutual work on the part of both partners. When we are openly giving, respect our own needs as well as our partner's needs and set healthy boundaries, we can expect to enjoy a relationship with a solid foundation.

Exercise

A Simple and Effective Self-love Practice

Love all of you and release the emotional charge of seemingly bad experiences of the past. Breathe deeply from the belly, hold it in while you make yourself the promise of loving all of yourself. Slowly let go of resentment and emotional charges of bad experiences of the past, and let your whole body become loose and relaxed. Do this a few times a day and see magic happen!

Notes

When you begin to love yourself, you will start to release some of your negative attachments, such as some people in your life, a job that does not support you, relationships, bad habits, unhealthy eating, and anything else that is not serving you. Anything that makes you feel small should go, if possible. This is self-love and it is a healthy and worthwhile practice that you should prioritize in your life.

Self-love also means having boundaries. It is not your job to fix other people's problems, to anticipate others' needs or to prioritize their needs above your own. It is OK to say no to anything that does not align with your values. It is your job to take care of your own needs first and then spread to others the love you feel inside. This is a healthy practice of love.

While it is not always possible to simply leave situations, people, jobs or family members who are not respectful and may hurt you with negative comments or judgments, the best approach is to become so self-loving and positive that nothing external can bring you down.

Love yourself, love nature, love humans, animals and the cosmos. The more you give love, the more love you will feel inside. This exchange of appreciation, joy and respect will give you a minty fresh feeling in your heart! You already know how to love. Just take a deep breath, expand your heart and exhale with love.

Exercise

Reset Before You Jump!

Just as you wash your hands before eating, clear your mind before engaging with the world. You prime your mind and body by meditation, affirmations, visualizing your future self, forgiving yourself and others. Before switching to another activity in your day, take a moment and breathe deeply through your nose, smile, and then exhale slowly through your nose. This will allow your body and mind to reset to positivity and to let go of tiredness, stress and negative emotional build-up from one aspect of your life to another. This form of self-care will benefit you and everyone else with whom you interact.

Notes

Social

We humans are social creatures and for centuries we have thrived in living with our tribes and our families and friends. Having a positive and friendly social environment and regularly meeting with people who make us happy, engaged and valued is wonderful for our well-being. We are hardwired to have social support and deep connection with others.

Who do you associate with? Who do you spend most of your time with? These are questions we need to raise regularly to assess our current social environment. Remember that energy is contagious and the people with whom we associate have a direct effect on our energy level, our well-being and our health. So it is extremely important to choose carefully who we spend time with.

It is worth mentioning that although we are social creatures and need to be with other people, we do *not* need to tolerate negativity, neglect, betrayal, abuse, bullying or any kind of negative behavior simply to have a social circle. Our circles are supposed to nurture us and help us grow, provide a supportive environment and bring joy to our lives. If your social circle doesn't do what it is supposed to do, then it's time to put it aside and declutter your social life from those who drag you down. This will help make room for new relationships. Build positive friendships that are filled with laughter, support, mutual learning and warm feelings. Stay away from negative vibes and people who don't support you.

On the other hand, whenever we engage in social settings, we need to carry positivity, joy and enthusiasm to both ourselves and everyone else. Each of us is responsible for bringing the best of ourselves to others, and for supporting, loving, energizing and nourishing others, as together we create an environment that promotes growth, calmness, joy and mutual respect.

Exercise

Journal What You Want in Your Social Life

Figuring out what kind of social life you want and what kind of people you want to associate with is the next piece to figuring out your life's grand vision. Write out details about what you want from your social life:

- What kind of friends and social circles do you want to have? What kind of relationships do you want to have?
- How do you want to spend time with your friends? What subjects do you want to talk about?
- What would you like to contribute to your social circles?
- What kind of work-related associations do you want to have?
- How do you want to communicate, support and love your loved ones?

Notes

Career, hobbies and passions

As we all know, an ideal career entails making money doing what you love. If you are already doing this, you are a successful person. And if you are not making money doing what you love and are not sure what your passion is, then go all the way back to the beginning of STEP 1 and re-read "What is your passion" to help you put yourself on the path of discovering and building your passion.

Like so many people, you are probably somewhere in between; you like your job well enough, but you also have passions, like playing a musical instrument, repairing sport cars, cooking, writing, dancing, playing sports, doing art projects, etc. If this is the case, feel grateful that your job enables you to have peace of mind about your basic needs while allowing you to do other things about which you are more passionate.

But never settle for a job in which you are not treated fairly and with respect, or one that wears you down or does not provide the growth you are looking for. I highly, highly recommend starting a side business related to one of your passions, one that you can grow over time. There is nothing better than making money off of your passion and without depending on someone else.

I put career, passion and hobbies under one category because I believe that you should go to work to do what you love to do, otherwise you will never be satisfied, and will always feel as if something is missing in your life. What you love to do might change over time and your career should change with it.

If your daily job is not based on your passion, but for now it gives you a comfortable life, you can take a different approach. Appreciate your job or career as a solid source of income but at the same time follow your passion on the side. If and when you are able to support your lifestyle doing what you love, you can make the switch, and if not, keep your passion alive regardless, and spend a few hours each week engaged in that passion. It will give you the fuel you need to build a successful life and feel fulfilled.

Exercise

So what are your hobbies? What activities, type of art or states of being bring you joy and satisfaction? Travel, music, animals, nature, science, spirituality, learning new skills... what do you desire?

Make your list and take action today to do what you are passionate about or feel pulled towards.

As far as your career, what do you want to work on? What kind of a place do you want to work in? Is it your business or do you work for someone else? What drives you? What kind of people do you want to work with?

Add all this to your journal!

Notes

Financials

Finances are different from careers. You might have a career you love, but not necessarily rely on it for building your wealth and financial freedom. No matter where your finances are today, you can improve them. Don't let your current reality steal your dreams. Your current reality is simply a collection of your choices from the past and how you behaved then. It has nothing to do with your future, unless you allow it to.

There is no lack of money, creativity and abundance in the world. The world is full of resources and we are the most creative creatures on this planet, able to create wealth and financial freedom for ourselves. We all have access to create a financially healthy life. Do not believe anyone who says there is not enough money, resources or new things to be built. That is simply not true. The creative power within us enables us to find resources, use the power of our imagination and create new things that other people find valuable and for which they will pay.

The secret to creating wealth is gratitude. That means developing and exercising an attitude of happiness and positivity with what you already have. This is definitely the opposite of what most people do when it comes to money and wealth. You might ask what being grateful has to do with financial abundance. Being grateful with what you already have while keeping your vision for your ideal future alive is a winning formula for success. When you are grateful for what you have in life and, let's face it, most of us have a lot to be grateful for, such as the sunshine, the roof over our head, our loved ones, the coffee we drink in the morning and the comfortable bed we sleep in, you become a positive person. You see a world full of hope, creativity and opportunity and your subconscious mind steers you toward what can bring you more joy, more of what you are already grateful for and what you desire. What you focus on expands - this is how your subconscious mind works.

It's your subconscious mind's job to find experiences, people and opportunities that match your state of being. So go ahead and count your blessings every day and feel happy about what you already have, while keeping the grand vision of your desired life alive in your mind.

A good life is about balance. As long as you spend, invest, and save in a balanced way, all is well. So learn about investment. Learn about different asset classes and find the ones you want to focus on, then keep learning by practicing and studying. Money is a game and working too hard for money is the worst way to achieve financial freedom or financial abundance. To make more money, you need to upgrade your mindset about it. Money has its own rules that you need to learn. Find out what limiting beliefs you have about money. Do you feel you have to work extra hard, betray your soul, become a selfish person or become a doormat for rich people if you yourself want to become rich one day? Have you been told that money does not grow on trees? How about "you need money to make money" or "You're not smart enough"?

Limiting beliefs and not understanding how money works are the main reasons for not having it. I have worked and interacted with many extremely rich people in my life and I know for a fact that the limitations we put on ourselves limit us from having financial success.

Money is a powerful tool. It is an amplifier. Money never really changes anyone. It just amplifies whoever you already are. If you are a generous person, money makes you more generous. If you are a person looking for ways to pull yourself up by bringing down others, money will help you do that to a greater degree. Money is neither good nor bad. It is a tool, just like a hammer, and how we use it is what's important. Therefore, it is vital that we examine our belief systems that came from our childhood and our family to discover what our subconscious mind believes about money.

If you grew up in a family that was always lacking, you may feel that having more money will require you to change who you are and you'll have to become a person you don't like, or you may believe that money is evil and that having more of it will attract problems and bad luck in your life. Or maybe you have been told that having more money requires you to work extra hard for many years and not enjoy your life. All of these are beliefs have been given to you by others but are not the truth.

Money is a tool to help us build a life we love. Invest, invest and invest. Take time to educate yourself on where to put your money so that it can work for you. Learning to invest is one of the best ways to create financial freedom and create the abundant life you always wanted. The key to investing is educating yourself, but the school system does not provide that education. While school provides knowledge in specialized fields, it is designed to generate skilled workers, not entrepreneurs and investors who desire an abundant life. So keep learning about money, investment and entrepreneurship. This will be an excellent use of your time because it will put you on course to better financial situations.

In my journey to figure out how the world works, what kind of people are happy, successful and joyful, I have met with many people who are very rich but are broken inside. Some of these people sold their souls, gained money by manipulating others, using people and gaining financial wealth without providing anything useful to society. I saw that these people suffer inside and have many mental issues that do not allow them to enjoy their riches. They live in daily torture and feel extremely alone and depressed inside, despite their seemingly happy, cheerful and confident appearance. So let's never go for these shortcuts that will break you inside and destroy you from within.

The truth is that we will only enjoy financial freedom and wealth if we provide to society something of which we are proud. We can only get rich when we help people get what they want or need. The more people you help with your products and services, the more money you will have. So learn the economics of scale and constantly ask yourself how you can provide more service to more people. Your subconscious mind will find ways to do it. Listen to your intuition when it speaks to you. Your intuition offers subtle ideas and suggestions that come to you suddenly, and seemingly out of nowhere. Write them down and take inspired actions immediately. Remember that being nervous and extra worried about money makes the situation worse. Easy does it!

I have often experienced that when I become anxious about making progress quickly, I push success away from me, but when I am relaxed and at ease, using my creative power, I can do amazing things.

Giving! In addition to gratitude, giving is another secret to attract wealth to you. Give with no expectations of return, give anonymously and visualize how excited the receiver might feel, and focus on how amazing you feel when you give. Giving without expectations and feeling love when you do it has incredible power. It will fill your life with joy, and will fuel the attitude of gratitude you are working to amplify in your life. Remember that positive attitudes attract joy and success like a magnet! So when you give with love, you will almost certainly get something back in some form, often from unexpected sources.

Take at least 30 minutes a day to upgrade your expertise in your field by reading articles, books, or listening to a podcast or audio books. This will level-up your game and will make you among the best in your field if done consistently.

Avoid busy and superficial work that wastes your time and ultimately your life. Train yourself to do meaningful work. This will give you joy and bring financial reward. If your day job is not something you feel passionate about, think of it as a secure source of income that allows you to do your real work on the side, or else change your job or profession. Do whatever it takes to find your fuel and be able to do something you feel a strong pull towards. Remove excuses and don't waste your time!

Exercise

What kind of financial success do you want in your life? How much money would allow you the lifestyle you want? Be specific so that your subconscious mind knows where to go when you assign the job to it!

Notes

Play, explore and take risks

Play like a child! Laughing, exploring new places and new ideas and meeting new people will surely help you feel alive again. We have been conditioned to be fearful and to play it safe but playing safe limits your life and causes you to repeat behavior even though you know what the outcome will be. There is no excitement or unpredictability in the known. But when you live a full life, you play, fall down, get back up and try it again, applying the lessons you learned from your previous failures. Much like a baby who is learning to walk; this is living. This is how life is supposed to be. Make rest, exploration, travel, getaways, play time and taking calculated risks all priorities in your life. Expand your comfort zone, because this is how you will expand your life and feel truly alive.

Our school systems tend to reward following orders and not failing. When you fail, you are considered unsuccessful and a concern for your teacher and parents. But in real life, playing too safe and not failing means you are not trying anything new. Were you born to follow rules and directions put in place by other humans who may not even be smarter than you?

Look for experiences that get your heart racing, give you belly laughs and fill your body with excitement. These experiences are everywhere; we simply need to relax our minds and remove the clutter of negativity in order to see them and take part in them!

We all have unique gifts and when we fulfill our mission, we feel good about ourselves. If you are not on the right track, you will feel stuck and a change should be in order.

Our number one priority should be to feel good. Whenever your vibration is low, and your thoughts are not positive or hopeful or beautiful, pause what you are doing and fix your emotional state before continuing. Our lives are much better and more joyful when every aspect is aligned; when our career and our hobbies are in harmony with our life vision and they support each other.

When I observed people with lots of money, I noticed how little respect they had for rules that had been put in place by others. I noticed that if they wanted something, they went after it, and literally did not take no for an answer. Bending rules and finding loopholes is one of the talents of financially successful people.

In fact, some rules are meant to be broken. I highly recommend examining any rules that block you.

Remember that all the rules you see in different environments are put in place by people who may not even be smarter than you. Those who understand this don't wait for other people to give them permission to execute on their dreams. These people make their own rules and do not wait for permission, or climb other peoples' ladders and seek approval from them.

My point is to take risks and try many doors, and if you are not allowed in, make your own door, make your own room, do whatever you need to do to "create" opportunities for yourself. It is rare for someone else to hand you a true opportunity; you need to create it for yourself. Keep knocking, keep building and keep hoping with a positive attitude, even when it seems as if you're not making meaningful progress. Soon, doors you hadn't thought about and opportunities you didn't know existed will show up in your life, if you keep your vision alive and your heart open so you can recognize them when they appear. Have a playful attitude toward life and keep going. There is only one requirement for you: add exploration, new learnings and discover uncharted territories to your daily life. When you fall down (because you will absolutely fall down if you're playing right!), figure out how to stand up quickly and without accumulating lasting negativity.

Exercise

Journal What You Want

What do you want to experience in your life? What places do you want to visit? Who do you want to meet? What do you want to work on next? What skills do you want to develop in the next 6 months, 12 months, 3 years? What activities make your heart feel minty fresh? How are you planning to include these joyful experiences in your daily life?

Notes

Exercise

Make a list of things that scare you but that you always wanted to do. Is it climbing a mountain, skydiving, swimming with dolphins, public speaking, trying a new kind of food, talking to strangers, etc.? Make a list of these and deliberately plan to include one thing that scares you into every day! Start with small things and build muscle. Over time you will notice you are more courageous and you are more open to trying new things.

And journal what you experience, what you tried and what you learned about yourself.

Notes

PART 2

CLIMB TO YOUR DESTINATION

STEP 4

MAKE IT ALL HAPPEN LIKE MAGIC

In the first 3 steps, we learned about the power of our minds and how our body and mind work together. We also journaled in great detail about the kind of life we want to create and about the grand vision for our lives. You should now have a clear picture of your future life written in your journal. **If you don't have this ready yet, stop here and go back to your notes or to STEP 1 and prepare your vision.**

If you are not trying to improve different aspects of your life on a daily basis, you are going backwards, because as we live, we accumulate pain, heartbreak, sabotage from others and ourselves, misfortune and bad luck that all, over time, pull us down unless we have a daily plan to combat them.

To grow, we must create a flow in the different areas of our lives. Flow means there is a balance of effortlessness and challenge. When your life flows without obstacles to stop it, there is synergy and everything falls into place at the right time.

STEP 4 is about applying magic to your true desires. This magic is unlocked using a power each and every one of us has but few of us know how to correctly use. This is the power of your imagination. As children, we imagine all the time, often daydreaming to the point where there is little distinction between reality and fantasy. But as we grow up, we use less of our imagination and rely more on logic and our analytical mind to solve our problems. I blame this on our school systems. We have been discouraged from daydreaming and have been prevented from using our imaginative powers the right way. Instead, we have been told to memorize material. This method of learning kills the most powerful tool we humans possess. It creates skilled workers who don't know how to create but who simply follow orders.

This is one of the best kept secrets in the wealthy and powerful families with whom I have interacted over the years. There is no tangible difference in the abilities of the people who use this astonishing power of imagination and those who don't. But so many of us are programmed not to recognize it or use it effectively to reach our goals. Whether or not this is by design, the point is that we all have this incredible power in us that can help us create fantastic results in our lives.

In STEP 2, we talked about how thoughts become real things. Thoughts and ideas are generated in our mind and when we get involved with them emotionally, our bodies have no choice but to act on them and make them a reality. In STEPS 1 through 3 we explored what we want most in life, and clarified for ourselves what we want to go after. Now it's time to apply the magic formula of locking what we want in our subconscious mind so it can go after it day and night and create what we want almost automatically. When you assign this job to your subconscious, much like radar it will find the right moves, the right places, the right people and the right opportunities to bring you closer to what you truly desire. Your inner knowing, your intuition and automatic responses to your environment will put you on the right path to achieve your goals when you choose to listen to your subconscious instead of ignoring it.

When you are relaxed, grateful for what you already have and feel happy, you are in your most creative state. This is because when your muscles relax, your mind enters a state of wonder; a state in which you are able to imagine your desired outcome and your desired future, and feel the emotions of that outcome. When it feels like you already have what you want to create, your brain creates new neural pathways that match your future desires. In other words, the path to your desired future is being physically created in your brain when you are in this state. It is pure magic! You use the power of your imagination to experience with your brain and body what it will feel like when you accomplish your desired future. You are basically programming your brain, body and subconscious mind to find a path for your desired outcome, so literally hardwiring your brain if you repeat it often enough. Astonishing, isn't it?

Now that we know imagination is our magical creative power, let's review some practical daily exercises to put it to work.

Vivid imagination generates strong emotions. Once you've learned how to use it wisely, it can transform your life in astonishing ways. Many of us use imagination the wrong way. We imagine things that we *don't* want to happen by imagining all the details, and then we get involved with it emotionally, which brings sadness, disappointment, worry and hopelessness to our present moment, blocking our creative power. This is the opposite of what we should do. Whatever you imagine with emotions, the subconscious mind will accept as reality. It has no way of knowing the difference between reality and imagination, so when you think negative thoughts, it projects negativity, worry, and fear into your environment, and we know that this causes you to act in certain negative ways.

When you feel negative emotions, you think more negative thoughts, and you react negatively to your environment and situations in your life. You become stuck in this negative loop that destroys your chances of creating a happy, joyful and successful life. Stop imagining things you don't want and start imagining what you do want. This does not mean that we should be wishful thinkers, ignoring danger and failing to prepare for it. Imagining what you don't want to happen is still a helpful practice. Imagine once or twice what could go wrong and make contingency plans to avoid or face problems that may occur... and then be done with it. Never go back to imagining bad outcomes multiple times or get involved with them emotionally and become worried and fearful. This will destroy your chances of success.

Your mind is a powerful tool that you need to learn how to use for your benefit. It has an amazing power to bring to reality what you imagine with intense emotions.

As most of us know, the brain works on patterns of recognition. This is why we recognize familiar faces. When something is unknown, we don't recognize it and when we don't recognize the "unfamiliar," we respond based on past conditioning, so anything new is stamped strange, scary, or even bad by our brain. But you can use your imagination to make your mind and body familiar with what you want in life. Be clear about how you want to feel when you have what you want, feel those emotions deeply now, and you'll create new "patterns of recognition" for your brain. When you are unclear about what you want, your brain will protect you from the unfamiliar, because, remember, one of its main goals is to keep you safe, and for the brain there is nothing scarier than the unknown.

Below are some practical tools and exercises that have been proven for centuries to work. These practices will help you use the power of your imagination to create the life you want. Remember, we are the co-creator of our lives and we must actively participate in it. We are not the product of our environment unless we allow ourselves to be.

Create a vision board

In step 3 we talked about a vision board but now it's time to dig deeper. A vision board is a piece of cardboard, a notebook, or even a digital file on your computer that contains images of things you want in life. What do you want to look like, how do you want to feel, what adjectives do you want to be associated with? Where do you want to live, what does success mean to you? All of these go onto your vision board.

Your vision board represents your vision and your dreams, so look at it a few times a day to remind yourself of your direction, and to give you the motivation and energy you need to focus, so you can concentrate on the right action and let go of distractions. I watched a very successful person who was extremely focused on his vision and it felt like nothing could stop him from getting what he wanted. *Nothing.* Once he set his eyes on his goal, he became unstoppable. I was fascinated to witness that. This is what a vision board should do, so keep it in your room, look at it every day and feel the emotions as if you already have everything on it, so your subconscious mind takes note. Remember, your subconscious thrives on repetition and its language is emotions.

Use the magical moment of your day

Right after you wake up in the morning, or when you are drowsy at night and ready to sleep, your brain produces alpha waves. In this state, you are relaxed and your analytical mind is quiet, while your subconscious mind is ready to absorb anything you give it... like a sponge. Use this time and this space to create the life you want. Bring the power of your imagination to these magical times of day. You have not only one but two of these sacred spaces every day in which to become who you are supposed to become. Use them!

Daily visualization exercise

Do the following as soon as you wake up and then again just before you fall asleep:

Close your eyes and start daydreaming… dream about the vision of your life; imagine yourself already living the future that you desire and feel the emotions that living that dream will bring. How do you walk, talk, engage with others in your dream. Imagine as much detail as you can! Notice that when you do this, you are feeling NOW how you want to feel in the future. **You are becoming that person at that moment**, you are programming your subconscious mind to go after this dream and build a path for you to get there. Now let the vision go while still holding on to those amazing feelings and go to sleep knowing that you will receive what you desired. Your subconscious mind never sleeps and it will tirelessly look for ways to achieve what you want!

A few words of warning: This is an extremely powerful tool to help you manifest what you desire. Use it with care and only desire things that are what you truly wish for and that are not based on resentment, hate, proving others wrong, or revenge. Using these exercises to manifest anything other than what truly brings you joy will put you on a wrong path that will bring with it deep depression, lack of self worth, extreme loneliness and a tortured soul. I have seen this in some very wealthy people who used the power of their mind to achieve financial success, but in the process they sold their soul. I have seen how they live in a hell of their own making.

Now put the details of how you felt and what you imagined in your journal. Repeat this exercise every day. It only takes a few minutes but it has an amazing impact on you and the likelihood that you will achieve your dreams.

Notes

Write down your goals and watch them come true

When you write things down, it makes you think more clearly and organize your thinking. Writing down your goal as if it has already come true and describing how it makes you feel has a powerful impact on your ability and commitment to achieve that goal. One amazing practice I recommend is to take a piece of paper, put your name on top of it and date it. Then start writing as if your desired life has already come true. Write down the details of your desired life and how you feel about it. Give this letter the date of when the dream life came true. Seal it and put it away, opening it only when your dreams have come true. To put your name on it and date it causes your subconscious mind to work hard to achieve what you have assigned to it. This is your promise to yourself! You might not get what you wanted on the exact date you specified, but rest assured that you will get it!

Don't worry about the future

Here is an unbelievable fact. Most of us spend a lot of our time remembering and thinking about past events or anticipating, worrying or thinking about the future. But the only time that truly exists is *now* and *now* is magical and precious. *Now* is the real life we have. For a few seconds, try to quiet your mind and truly be in the moment. You see how *now* is calming, special and magical? **Enjoy *now* while you are working toward your future.** We should never sacrifice now for a long period of time as we are building the future we want. We attract who we are, so if we live our life now in a way that is far from the future we want to build by over working, worrying, and having negative thoughts and feelings, we are getting farther away from what we want to attract in our lives.

From time to time, we all have to do things that are not aligned with our passion, but the majority of our time should be filled with enjoyable activities, enjoyable learning and enjoyable social circles, so that we can feel and radiate the emotions of love, joy, growth, expansion, satisfaction and gratitude. We know that these emotions are what motivate us, attract what we desire in our lives and help us build the future we want as we enjoy the *now*.

Worry disables you, makes your body tense and prone to cold, flu and diseases. Worry does nothing useful and it steals the power, the beauty and the magic of *now*. Did you know that most of what we worry about never comes true? So stop worrying and find flow in your days, where you become unstuck and can free yourself. This is where and when you are growing and enjoying life... with a balance of ease and challenge.

Exercise

How to Live in the *Now*

A few times a day, find a calm and quiet place, breathe deeply, and exhale slowly. Pay attention to your breath and watch how it flows throughout your body with ease and without a struggle. Notice how it calms your mind, warms your stomach, relaxes your shoulders and neck and opens your heart.

Another exercise is to take long walks in nature. Breathe deeply and notice the birds, the trees, the leaves and how the sun feels on your skin. Notice the earthy smell of nature and feel the soil or the grass under your feet. This practice will energize you and will cement you in the *now*.

At first, you might only live in the *now* for short periods of time, but as you continue practicing and paying attention to the patterns of your thoughts, and try to change them when they are traveling to the past or future, you will eventually notice that you live more in the *now* and that your days are calmer and flow more gently.

Notes

Stop rehearsing the past events in your mind

A majority of our thoughts every day are negative and it is astonishing that most of our thoughts are also repetitive. Most of what we think today was what we thought yesterday and the day before and the day before that. Our minds love repetition and staying in a closed loop and in the known. This is because we have given this power to our minds. If we let it, our mind will take over our life and we will become a slave to it, repeating and repeating the same thoughts and experiences again and again. Our mind is a powerful tool but it is just that... a tool. As long as we identify ourselves with this tool and believe everything it tells us, we are its slave.

When we allow the mind to rehearse and remember a negative past experience, and become emotionally involved, it is as if we have that bad experience over and over again instead of the one time it actually happened. Repeating it will destroy your happiness, your mood, and it will weaken your immune system so you will be more prone to sickness. When you repeat these experiences in your mind, you are programming your mind and literally installing neurological pathways in your brain to live that experience over and over again. In other words, you are literally changing who you are, and for the worse! I have seen this in real life. You don't want to go there. Trust me.

How to stop thinking about the past

In order to stop this cycle, we need to first build awareness and notice our thought patterns - regular meditation and mindfulness practices do just that. When we start to notice these negative thoughts coming into our mind, we are already breaking the cycle. We can now choose not to engage with them. And the best way to not become engaged with them is to notice them rather than push them away, because when we push them away, they come back stronger. These thoughts are actually negative energies trapped in your body that want to be released. They will come back again and again until you set them free. There are many ways to do this and below I will show you what has worked best for me.

When you notice a negative thought emerge, acknowledge it. Don't engage with it but instead open your arms and give it a big hug. You can literally open your arms or else do it figuratively in your mind, breathe deeply and wait until it resolves itself. It is a deeply satisfying feeling when you feel this negative energy dissolve in your awareness. The same negative thoughts and memories might show up again but every time you engage in this practice, they will be less intense, until they completely dissolve and never return.

STEP 5

BECOME THAT PERSON NOW

In this step I want to talk about something that we hear about all the time, but that so many don't understand and don't know how to implement in their lives. As I worked with and observed successful people, I saw how applying this particular tool in their daily life amplified their success. I have also seen how misusing this powerful magic can destroy lives, behaving like an internal weapon, breaking down the individual who is misusing it. I rely on you to use this power with care, self-respect, and personal responsibility. So let's learn what it is I'm talking about.

At its base, everything is energy. Everything vibrates. Even the most solid objects vibrate at quantum level. And everything in the world has a *different* vibration. Different people vibrate differently and this is why you hear people referring to someone's 'vibe.' We radiate vibrations to the environment around us and, much like a magnet, whatever we radiate attracts back things that are in harmony with those vibrations. So to truly change our lives and get the results we desire in life, we need to change our vibration to match our desires. This is a secret that, if we get right, will transform our lives.

So let's talk about vibration in detail and in a more practical way so we can apply it to our journey and reach STEP 5.

How to change your vibration

Let's say your goal is to become a successful business owner. You need to vibrate in a business owner's vibration. The energy you vibrate (your vibe) creates your attitude toward life, toward other people, the way you think, the way you talk, walk, write and the way your entire life operates. Your vibration needs to be in tune with a successful business owner's vibration if you want to become a successful business person. The successful business person's vibrations dictate what she does, how she thinks about business, how she talks, what plans she makes for the business, how well she sleeps, etc.

This means you should study people who inspire you and already have what you desire. Try to associate with them, find mentors who are where you want to be in life, watch their videos, read their books and learn how they talk, how they analyze a situation, how they spend their time. Watch what actions they take, listen to how they think about business and life and discover what skills they have that you are missing. Then try to emulate these behaviors. Talk like them, walk like them, think like them, and when you try to solve a problem, ask yourself how the person you are trying to emulate would think about this problem and try to cultivate the skills you are missing. The answers will come to you.

Do this every day, and over time you will become this person and will generate and attract success. This is what it means to vibrate at the level of your desire. Without becoming the person who attracts and generates and creates what you want, you will never reach your goal, and even if you get what you want, it will be temporary and you will lose it. So become the person now!

This brings me to an important point - and the biggest contribution I can offer you in this book. It is a gift from my heart and soul to yours, and here it is: Before you fully commit to the person you decide to emulate, study them. See what kind of person they are. What are their values? How do they work and do they respect other people, especially those who seem to have nothing to offer them? How do they treat the janitor, the maid, the laborer? How do they talk about other people? Are they genuine in the values they demonstrate?

When someone shows you once that they are faking it, believe them!

You don't want to emulate people who you later find out are fake. Don't make these people your ideal. In fact, never make anyone your ideal. After all, everyone has issues, problems and a dark side. So instead, decide what skills you want to develop and find people who have what you want and have those skills, then emulate only those specific skills.

Look at the description of the person you want to become that you developed in STEP 1 and 3. In detail, figure out what skills you need to develop in order to become that person. DECIDE to become that person today and develop yourself on a daily basis. Soon you will become the person you desire to be.

This does not mean pretending to be rich, lying about your abilities or deceiving others. If you choose this route, you are betraying your soul and your body, and it will eventually come back to haunt you. I have seen this happen again and again with con artists and people who are looking for a quick way to get rich by deceiving, manipulating and using others. It never works. You might get what you want but you will either lose it or will never enjoy it. Whatever you put out in the world will come back to you. Trust me, I have seen it again and again.

Exercise

An Incredibly Quick and Effective Way to Become the Person You Want to Become

Dr. Vladimir Raikov was a Russian neuropsychologist in the 1970s who developed a simple technique (now called the Raikov Effect) that helps people take on the skills and talents of people they model themselves after in just a few minutes. His client's performance levels transformed to those of Picasso, Einstein, Mozart, and other geniuses. I have tried this method with skills that I wanted to develop and I was transformed within a few minutes. No other course, book or advice has had this magical effect on me. I am confident that it will help you fast track skills that you want to develop to become the person you want to be. Let's learn more about the Raikov Effect.

1. Choose a skill you want to develop. For example, public speaking, having more charisma, becoming a great writer, being more creative, etc.

2. Find a person who has the skill you want. If you cannot find someone, imagine your future self with that skill.

3. Close your eyes and take 10 deep breaths. Relax your body and focus on how the breaths move in your body. Let go of anything else and just be with your breaths.

4. Now imagine the person who has the skill you want to develop in yourself and watch them demonstrate that skill. Watch how they do it, how they breathe, how they walk and carry themselves.

5. Walk to that person, who is happy to meet you and smiles. Take their brain and put it in your head.

6. Feel the rush of energy in your body.

7. Your breathing changes, your posture changes, you feel that skill has been transferred to you by this person. Breathe and accept this gift.

Notes

STEP 6

GET OUT OF YOUR OWN WAY

Now that we know what we want out of life, we know who we want to be. We are motivated. We are committed and we march forward and no one can stop us and the world is amazed at our commitment and sense of purpose. But you hear a voice inside of you saying, *What if I fail, what if they laugh at me? Who am I to have big dreams like this? How will I recover if I fail? I don't have the knowledge, the experience, I am too old, I am too young, other people are more qualified than me*, etc. This voice is a blocker that self-sabotages your success. But why is this voice there in the first place? Where does it come from? Is it your intuition? Is it your fears? Is it your soul trying to protect you? Let's find out.

Limiting beliefs

In STEP 2 we talked about how all of us have limiting beliefs that have been downloaded to our subconscious before age 7 and are also from the environment in which we live. We all have biases and beliefs that are not rooted in reality. Beliefs are simply thoughts that we have accepted because we have been told they are true or they are thoughts we gave to ourselves by assigning specific meaning to past events in our life. For example, a child who has the experience of being laughed at and humiliated at school might believe that they are not good enough and as a result they feel shame inside.

Beliefs enable us to quickly make sense of the world, how it works and what is beneficial or harmful to us, and we do need beliefs in order to operate successfully in the world. The problem is that some of our beliefs limit our abilities to create the life we want. In our subconscious mind we might have beliefs like, *I am not good enough, I don't deserve success, Life is unfair, I have to give up honesty, love, joy, or my family in order to get rich, I am too old to start over, I am too young and no one will trust me, I don't have a formal education*, and so on.

It is necessary for us to realize that these are all limiting beliefs. If you look, you will find plenty of examples in the world of people who felt some of these same "lacks" that you feel, but despite that, they achieved what they wanted to achieve. You might think they have simply been lucky. But this is also a limiting belief! Who says you cannot get lucky as well, who says you cannot create your own luck?

We all have doubts and limiting beliefs but people who go after what they desire and eventually become who they want to become do not let these beliefs stop them. Once you recognize that the limiting beliefs are just thoughts with no concrete truth, you are already on your way to removing them and replacing them with positive and enabling thoughts and beliefs like, *I, too, can do it, I, too, can become who I want to become.* As long as you go after your deepest desires instead of what society has hypnotized you to believe were measures of success, happiness and a good life, you can create what you want.

Limiting beliefs act like hidden blockers in your life, stopping you, sabotaging you and slowing you down from becoming who you are supposed to become. If you feel you have done your best multiple times and still are unable to manifest your true desires, then you likely have limiting beliefs that are blocking you. In other words, at the energy level, your vibration does not match the goal you want to achieve. So you either need to change your goal or change your vibration. If what you want is your deepest desire and you feel a strong connection to it and have been wanting it for many years, then removing your beliefs and replacing them with new, empowering ones will do wonders for you.

But if in the middle of pursuing your dream you realize it is not what you want after all, and you have accomplished it to simply to appear successful in society's eyes, or because of what your parents or someone else wanted, then I highly encourage you to go through the steps in this book to find your true desire. It's simple, if you are living a life that is not based on your true desire, you will not be happy, and will not experience deep and lasting joy.

Now that we know we need to work on limiting beliefs if we want to embark on the path to our destination, I will show you practical ways to change your life from deep inside. Remember that inner growth comes first, and without removing the weeds from inside, we cannot see the seeds of our desires flourish.

Self-hypnosis

We are all hypnotized in one form or another. In early childhood, before the age of seven, our analytical mind is not yet developed. What we have is mostly the subconscious mind, and whatever goes in there is absorbed like a sponge without being questioned. That's like being hypnotized. Anything that goes into your subconscious and becomes part of you determines what you believe and how you automatically behave. We are also hypnotized by our environment; what we see, hear and have been told on a regular basis causes us to believe it. We are hypnotized by our environment to accept without question what is good, what is accepted, what is considered success and what we are capable of.

But what if we could hypnotize ourselves to remove the limiting beliefs we have inside and replace them with what enables us to create a truly joyful life? What if we could take these hidden blocks that exist inside of us and smooth the path that leads to where we want to go and who we want to become? If we could do these things, then there would be no stopping us! And the good news is that we absolutely can do them, and here's how:

Remove Limiting Beliefs Self-Hypnosis

Repeat this exercise for at least 30 days, 15 minutes a day

- Lie down in a calm and relaxing place
- Close your eyes and take deep and long inhales, making sure your belly rises first then your chest, and exhale slowly. Repeat this 10 times.
- Relax the muscles on your face, imagine your eyes, your mouth, your cheeks all sinking into deep relaxation. Move to your neck, shoulders, arms, chest, back, heart, stomach, hips, legs and toes and relax all your muscles by breathing deeply while reciting, "relax your arms," "relax your stomach," etc.
- Now imagine the person you want to become, and the characteristics that this person has. For example, *I am calm, I am positive, I am smart. I am a good communicator. I am helping my clients, I am wealthy, I am healthy*. Imagine your future self. See her walking, talking to people, closing business deals, laughing and enjoying life and demonstrating the qualities you want to have.
- Hold onto this image for about five minutes and when you are ready, slowly open your eyes.

Notes

Congrats, you just hypnotized yourself into being what you desire instead of what others hypnotized you to become! The deeper the hypnosis session, the less resistant you'll be to accepting the suggestions from your subconscious mind and the quicker the change in belief and behavior.

Get rid of harmful stress

Let's dig a little deeper into our nervous system, as it is important to understand how it functions. Our nervous system greatly influences our ability to create the life we want. What our nervous system does is pure magic and when we know how to use and direct it, we are on our way to having healthier, more capable, stronger bodies. Our nervous system also directly affects our mood, stress levels, happiness and the joy we feel and how we respond to the environment in which we live. I think of our nervous system as our roots. Plants grow roots in the soil and I believe we humans grow roots inside ourselves. The stronger your roots, the more nourished life you'll have. As a matter of fact, scientists recently discovered that there are surprising similarities between plant cells and neurons in our bodies. Neurons are special nerves in the nervous system that transmit signals between different parts of the body.

Part of your nervous system is called the autonomic nervous system, which unconsciously regulates the body's functions, such as digestion, respiratory rate, pupillary response, urination, sexual arousal and heart rate. The autonomic nervous system (ANS) has two branches called sympathetic - the fight, flight, freeze response - and parasympathetic - rest and digest.

The sympathetic branch of your nervous system is activated when you perceive danger. The danger could be real, such as a hungry lion ready to attack you, or it could be perceived, such as imagining being fired from work and not being able to provide for yourself or your family. This sympathetic system is commonly known as the 'fight, flight or freeze' response. This means that when you feel you are in danger, you either prepare to fight, run away or freeze like a lizard. This is how we respond to stress. Our muscles tighten, our pupils enlarge and we become hyper-focused in order to deal with the huge stressor in front of us. But the other system in our body that is the opposite of fight, flight and freeze is the parasympathetic system, or the 'rest and digest' response. It is activated when we feel relaxed and safe, ready to enjoy life.

These two branches of the autonomic nervous system (ANS), sympathetic and parasympathetic, are both very useful systems in our bodies and we need both to be able to respond to great stressors in our lives and to be able to enjoy life. The problem arises when we become too stressed out. The fight, flight and freeze response is supposed to be activated when a true life-threatening situation occurs, not when we live our daily life. In many cases, people live in work environments that are too stressful for our bodies to handle so the sympathetic nervous system becomes hyper-activated. Life doesn't have to be this way. It is our limiting belief that forces us to kill ourselves, overwork ourselves or tolerate extremely stressful daily life in order to get ahead. I have seen extremely successful people on the outside with large houses, expensive cars and millions in the bank, or fancy titles and positions at top companies who are miserable because they chose this route.

When we put ourselves in continuously stressful situations, we lose balance in our body, which can make us ill. You are not able to be creative and to focus on your long-term goals or your life's vision when dealing with daily stress because your body is focused on the dangers it feels at the moment and eliminates everything else so it can help you survive. So the number one thing to do is to eliminate unnecessary stress in your life so that you can have the room to create the life you want. You'll recall that STEP 3 was about decluttering your environment, your social groups and your work environment. Anything that does not speak to your future self will fade away automatically when you focus on the life you want to create. Make sure you truly declutter your life from unnecessary stress, overwork and negative environments, and if you are not able to change your environment right away, at least change how you respond to it.

Now I want to show you a few very practical exercises you can do on a daily basis to regulate your nervous system and stimulate the parasympathetic nervous system to create calm and serenity inside you so that you can clean your body and mind from stress. The end result of these exercises is to become more creative, more capable and confident to go after the life you desire!

Vagus nerve is your friend

It is a known fact that physical well being and emotional well being are deeply connected. For instance, when you have a headache, it is hard to feel cheerful and joyful, and on the other hand, when we have a good night's sleep, some exercise, sunshine, and healthy food, we are happier, more cheerful and ready to be socially engaged.

What most of us don't know is that there is a nerve in our nervous system called the vagus nerve, which is the tenth nerve in the nervous system and one of the most amazing, magical ones responsible for our physical and emotional well-being. A branch of this nerve starts in your brain and goes all the way to your gut, touching every organ along the way, including the heart, lungs, kidneys, liver and pancreas. The job of this vagus nerve is to activate your parasympathetic system, the rest and digest response that causes your mind and body to relax, enjoy life and help you become socially engaged. When this magical nerve is stimulated and toned, you will enjoy life and will feel great, so you can be spontaneous, responsive, happy, engaged, cheerful and in the moment in your social interactions.

Below are some practical tools and exercises to help you tone your vagus nerve. I encourage you to incorporate at least a couple of these tactics in your daily routine for best results:

1. Connect to your dreams and deepest desires

   It is amazing that your physiology actually needs to connect to its deepest desires in order to feel vibrant, healthy and positive. When we are connected to our desires and remind ourselves on a daily basis where we are going, our root, aka our vagus nerve, in particular, takes note and starts to be toned, healthy and strong.

2. Cold shower

   At the end of your daily shower, expose your body to cold water for 10 seconds or more. This practice engages and tones your nervous system. A cold shower releases the sense of depression and sadness and immediately recharges your life batteries!

3. Regularly walking in nature, swimming, moderate physical exercise

   Daily moderate exercise that does not put your body under too much stress is the best form of exercise. When you move your body, your circulation improves, and your body produces hormones associated with joy and well-being so you feel more confident, happy, and joyful. This means your mind is open to learning more and looks for opportunities to help you get closer to your goals.

4. Daily yoga practice

   Yoga is more than a form of exercise. If done right, it can transform you from inside out, engaging your soul, mind and body. It is a complete healing system. If you choose to do yoga, I recommend you focus on it from a holistic perspective, and not confuse it with complex stretches and balancing poses. Study what it means to be a yogi and how someone who genuinely practices yoga thinks, behaves and processes thoughts and events. Yoga is a journey worth taking!

5. 5-2-8 breathing

   Breathe deeply from your belly for five seconds, hold it and count two seconds, then slowly release it for eight seconds. Repeat this five times before you engage with the world, before your meetings at work, before you switch from one activity to the next. This is an easy way to tone and activate your vagus nerve and change the state of your mind to a more positive, socially-engaged, strong and flexible one. This simple exercise, when done daily, can improve your attitude, and we know now that having a positive attitude is your ticket to creating a better life!

6. Make some noise

   Singing, humming, chanting, and gargling will stimulate the vagus nerve by activating the muscles at the back of the throat and vocal cords connected to the nerve. So go ahead and make some noise!

7. Social connections

   Laughing with friends and family, spending positive time with people you like and hugging them are great ways to soothe your nervous system.

While doing these exercises and practices are soothing, relaxing and activate the vagus nerve and therefore your parasympathetic system, it is important to note that these techniques will not resolve the underlying anxiety and stress you feel. These techniques should be used to calm you down so that you can think about what to do to attack the stress and anxiety at its core and definitively solve the problem. It might mean leaving a job that no longer supports and serves your needs, leaving behind friends and social connections who are negative and don't support your future self, or simply putting practical boundaries in place to protect your energy and your well-being.

The fire ceremony

Every month - to begin with, do this every day for 30 days, then do it once a week, then do it once a month from then on. Write down what you don't like about yourself and what you have been told by others that you feel is holding you back in life and then offer it to a fire. Watch the paper burn and tell yourself, "It is all gone now." Then immediately say with conviction the opposite of these negative thoughts. Smile and feel that what was not serving you is burned in the fire and the energy of it is changed to heat and light, bringing its warmth and light to you.

For example, write on a piece of paper "I am not not enough and I need to work extra hard to be valuable." Offer it to the fire and watch how it burns and changes to light and heat. Then replace it with, "I am whole. I am enough and I bring value to the table. My perspective matters."

Believe it, feel it, see it in your mind's eye.

Repetition

Wake up early, have an hour a day to yourself

Repetition is another way we can influence our subconscious mind. The more we do something, the more it becomes part of who we are. Repetition is how habits are formed. They say we build habits and habits build us. This means that once a habit is formed, we mostly do it automatically without thinking too much about it. It takes about 60-90 days for a habit to form, and about a year to stick, so the more you repeat something, the more it becomes who you are. Habits are our way to install and automate behaviors we want to have.

So go back to your notes and vision boards from STEP 5, where you decided who you want to be. Remember that your desired life needs to match who you are. Become like the person who has the life you want and there is no way that you won't have your desired life. What kind of habits does the person you want to become have? How does he spend his day?

Our days are miniatures of our lives. So how you spend your day is how you spend your life.

Repeat on a daily basis the actions, the thoughts and the behaviors of the person you want to become and your desired life will become your actual life!

It is very important to build a ritual for yourself. Start your day with an hour to yourself and ground yourself by connecting to your life's vision, exercising a bit, journaling and processing thoughts and feelings, making important decisions and reading a few pages to learn something new that aligns with your vision. This tranquility hour will make your day go smoothly, stress-free and purposeful, and when the inevitable stresses come your way, you will know how to effectively respond. If you start your day answering emails, engaging with social networks, checking your messages and doing everything else that is required of you, you are in reactive mode, taking care of everyone else's agenda instead of your own dreams and desires. So go ahead, wake up an hour earlier each day and ground yourself and connect to who you want to be. This is a magic formula that will put you on a winning path.

Did you say hi to your inner child today?

Have you ever noticed how some parts of our personalities never change? What made you fearful and joyful is still in you as an adult.

We all have an inner child. It is the child version of ourselves who never grows up and still lives inside of us. This child has needs that are unmet, has fears, hopes and dreams. This child has had life experiences that were less than perfect and those feelings are trapped and carried inside as trauma. We are now the parent of this child, and it is our job to take care of their needs and help them pass through their fears and go toward their goals.

The inner child is a psychological concept to describe who we were before puberty. What this child learned, experienced and wanted is still inside of us. When we connect deeply to this child, and see her wants, needs and who she is, we can connect to our deepest desires, see the childhood traumas, or psychological wounds that most of us have in some form, and start the healing process that transforms us. As part of our self-care, it is our responsibility to make sure our inner child is happy, well and seen by us. Because when we don't take care of our deepest needs, we show up stressed, unhappy, jealous, angry and disengaged with the world around us and this is when we hurt others. We might even hurt our closest friends or family members, not because we want to, but because we act on behalf of the hurt child within.

This is why loving ourselves and taking care of our own needs is the best way we can help others. Self-care is not a selfish act but a responsibility we each have to heal ourselves so that we don't transfer to others the negative feelings we feel inside. Remember that hurt people hurt people. It is worth mentioning that this is why we need to forgive people who hurt us, as they acted from their own past trauma and they simply transferred the hate, anger, and abuse to us in order to feel some temporary relief.

Work on forgiveness and focus on yourself and your own needs to heal your inner child and love yourself so much that the overflow of love can heal the people around you. You cannot help anyone else until you put your oxygen mask on first.

Talk to your inner child

To calm and parent your inner child, I recommend talking to her whenever she feels scared, lonely, ashamed, worried and anxious. Check in with your inner child often and make sure she is happy, seen and taken care of.

This is how I talk to my inner child whenever she is nervous and scared when I do something that has been scary for me:

> *I am here with you. I see you, I hear you and I love you. You and I will go along the path of life together holding each other's hands. Hold my hand, trust me and let's go together. I see your fears, your love and your passion. Let me take you there. To where you belong, where your gifts come alive and you are the happiest. Hold my hand and let's go together. This is our turn, our chance and these are our dreams. I am with you all the way. Let's go together!*

Visualize the open door on top of a cliff

Sometimes our negative past experiences bother us. They come to our mind automatically and we choose to engage with them and repeatedly feel the painful emotions brought on by them. Our experiences will make us stronger, wiser and more successful if we learn the lesson and let go of the negative emotional charge associated with bad experiences. Here is how to do this:

Exercise

Let Go of the Past

- Find a comfortable place and close your eyes.
- Take a few deep inhales and slow exhales and feel calm and relaxed.
- Now imagine yourself on top of a cliff, and you are looking at a big, beautiful gate. The gate is open and bright white light shines through it. This door is your gateway to your future.
- Look down the cliff, and see all your memories, experiences and the people in your life, including the people who hurt you and wronged you.
- These people have been building a cliff for you all along. They have been moving you to your destination without knowing it.
- Take a good look at these people, EACH of whom is holding a rock above their head. They are using these rocks to build the cliff on which you are standing, in front of this beautiful shiny gate.

Notes

This exercise will help you make sense of every event and experience in your life and understand how each one brought you to this point and made you ready to build your desired life.

Forgiveness

Forgiveness is one of the most powerful things you can do to free yourself, bring joy to your life and improve all aspects of your life. When you genuinely forgive people who have hurt you, your relationships, sleep quality, peace of mind, creativity, and focus all improve many times over. Forgiveness brings real freedom and real internal lightness within.

Anyone who has done anything that has bothered you has done so because of their own past experiences, their own physical and mental wounds that have triggered and conditioned them to act and respond in a certain way. Remember that hurt people hurt people. When someone hurts you, always remember how much hurt they went through that they are now bringing to you. The pain they feel that made them behave the way they did toward you is to blame, not the person. I know it is very hard to forgive some people, but keep in mind that forgiving does not mean letting someone off the hook for their wrongdoings nor does it mean forgetting about the past. It certainly does not mean you need to remain in touch with the person who hurt you and tolerate their future maltreatment. Forgiveness means setting yourself free so you can move on.

In fact, I encourage you to stay away from people who continuously hurt you without meaningful improvement on their part. There is no good reason to be someone else's emotional trash dump and allow them to release their negative emotions on you. It is your responsibility to care for yourself and block people who are not in good mental health. You will never change them. So block them from your life, put boundaries in place and continue on your own path. Forgiving truly improves your mental and physical well-being. It is an extremely powerful force that truly changes you for the better.

Forgiveness lowers your heart rate, lowers blood pressure, and is a great stress reliever. It can also reduce fatigue and improve sleep quality. Psychologically speaking, forgiveness will eliminate the negative experience of stress and inner conflict and at the same time will help you restore positive feelings, behaviors, and thoughts that are your natural state of being.

Forgiveness Exercise

Put yourself in a calm mental state. Take a hot Epsom salt bath, or sit in a semi-dark room with calming music and candles. Close your eyes, breathe deeply through your belly 10 times. Bring to your mind someone who hurt you, see them in front of you and look them in the eye. Say, "I forgive you! You were in pain; that is why you hurt me. And I forgive myself." Breathe deeply a few more times and feel negative charges leave your body and mind. Repeat this exercise every day until you truly forgive that person, then move on to the next one.

You'll know when you have truly forgiven someone, because you'll no longer feel negative emotions associated with the memories of those past negative experiences that hurt you.

Notes

Forgive Yourself

We also need to forgive ourselves. We did what we were able to do at the time. Maybe we used a coping mechanism that we no longer approve of. That means we have grown and that is something to celebrate. So forgive your past mistakes; you did your best with what you knew and were capable of. If you had known better, you would have done better. So forgive yourself and feel the powerful magic this brings to your life.

Gratitude

Being thankful and grateful for what we already have opens a path to receive more. People who complain all the time, are envious of others and feel like victims of circumstance block their own progress, devalue their own inner gifts, feel resentful, stressed and unhappy. We know that these feelings put you in a negative cycle of thinking the wrong thoughts, that thoughts create emotions in your body, and that your body acts on these emotions.

So if you are not grateful for the small things that you have in life, such as a comfortable bed to sleep in, someone to love, morning coffee, the flowers you see from your window, your health and anything else you already have, you will radiate negativity and remember, what you radiate you will attract back to you. It is important to see the good in your life. Unappreciative people become unlucky people and appreciative and positive people become lucky.

Exercise

Daily Gratitude

Every morning as soon as you wake up and every night before you sleep, take a few minutes and count your blessings. What are you thankful for? Feel the gratitude and the smile it brings to your face and notice how it changes your breath and opens your lungs to receive more. This is what gratitude does. It makes you receptive to more!

Notes

STEP 7

SURRENDER AND THEN TAKE THE RIGHT ACTIONS

The bird that got stuck

The patio of our house has a deep high ceiling that confuses the birds that fly under it. Birds often fly up toward the deep ceiling and get stuck there! They fly east, west, north and south, but they can't find any way out. They work harder, fly faster, and then become nervous and scared, and as a result they hit the corners of the ceiling. They do this so many times that they become exhausted and hurt and eventually SURRENDER. As they do this, they fly down from the ceiling and are able to see the sky outside and find their way out of the patio.

When I watch them do this, it occurs to me how so many of us do the same thing. We work too hard, try too much, and feel stuck, unable to make meaningful progress in our lives. The stress seeps in as we try even harder and harder. Just like the birds that get stuck in the deep ceiling of the patio, we cannot find our way out or see solutions. We need to stop trying so hard and exhausting ourselves, and instead relax and surrender while keeping our big goal in mind. When we do this, we are able to see clearly and find new ways to reach our destination.

How to surrender

We often try to control our environment and the way things are, and that's when anxiety sets in. We feel helpless when we are not able to control things that happen in the world around us. What someone else does, how they think, and what actions they take become a source of anxiety for us. Remember that the only thing we have full control over is ourselves, our bodies, our mind and the thoughts on which we choose to focus. When we let go of controlling the events and the people around us and expecting them to fit into our own beliefs and the way we see the world, we become more conscious of our internal world, which is our bodies, the sensations we feel, our thoughts and our state of being. This is the world we have control over.

When fear creeps in, notice it and breathe into it without trying to push it away. When you pay attention to it, and you accept it as your current state of being, you can surrender and accept the world outside of yourself as it is. This is the place you see new possibilities and new ways to get to your destination. Pushing and working too hard to the point of exhaustion doesn't help you. Instead, relax, accept things as they are, and be present in the moment so that you see the many possibilities in front of you. In other words, don't be too narrowly focused on one way of doing things. Let go of your control of the environment, see things as they are and expand your focus. This is when you become creative and are able to find new paths to your destination that were not previously visible to you.

I am a big believer in the 80/20 rule when it comes to manifesting goals and dreams, which in this context means that 80% of your results come from 20% of your efforts. I have experienced time and time again that I worked extra hard for a specific goal for quite some time, but ultimately realized that most of what I did did not actually matter and was only "busy work," so could have easily been skipped. My time could have been directed toward family and friends, self care, learning new skills or simply more sleep and rest. The outcome would have been the same or even better if I hadn't worked or tried so hard.

I observed when working with many successful people that they never became extra busy or overworked themselves to the point of exhaustion - except when a push was needed to finish up a project or a milestone, launch something new that they had been working toward for a long time or other *occasional* situations. But in most cases, easy, calm and calculated moves do the trick!

Don't fill your days with a huge to-do list, tasks and activities. This is called 'busy work', not productive work that will take you to your destination. It is better to say no to meaningless work and say yes more often to new possibilities, new ways of doing things and things you haven't tried before.

So don't work too hard and never run yourself down. Relax, see things as they are, accept where you are in life without fighting it. This is when you will automatically find a new path and take the actions that will take you to where you want to be.

STEP 8

KEEP GOING

STEP 8 is the last step to creating an amazing life, but it is not actually a step. It is a reminder to always get back up when you fall down.

Many people do one or two of the steps in this book and, amazingly, they still see some success in their lives, and this separates them from those who have no dreams and no vision for their lives. I have seen many successful people who have implemented a couple of these steps and they have created a life that is a dream for many others. I have also seen people who have tried to create shortcuts or tricks to gain fast financial success by manipulating others and have seen how unhappy, lonely and dissatisfied they become on the inside. Using others for your own benefit will never result in a well-rounded and joyful life. My recommendation is to do the deep work that is necessary to create a life you can truly enjoy, while the overflow of your joy, self-love and self-respect inspires and helps others.

If you love yourself, you will never manipulate others, because you would be betraying yourself and your basic human needs of making connections with others and being true to yourself. Your body feels the pressure and the pain when you try to use others and it becomes rigid like a rock, creating pain, illness, mental disorders and other major problems in daily life. Why take the manipulative approach when it will never give you the life you want? Why not heal your mind and body, free yourself from past trauma that controls your behavior and create a beautiful, joyful life that will bring you and the people in your life joy, happiness and lasting success? You can absolutely create this life!

Fail, get back up and keep going

What is failure? Failure simply means that you tried something and it did not work. There could be many reasons why something doesn't work out. Let's separate failure into four different categories and expand on them:

1. The idea was not your true desire

   We learned in STEP 2 that in many cases we have been programmed by others about what success looks like and we bought into other people's ideas about how our life should unfold. When we fail time and time again, it could be that the goals and visions we have chosen for ourselves may not be based on our true desires and our natural gifts, and the truth is that we will keep failing if our deepest desires are not in agreement with the vision we set out for ourselves.

Remember that you need to become the person who attracts the goals and desires you want to manifest in your life and the person you need to become, so if you are not in harmony and in love with the person you want to become, then there will be internal conflict, you will sabotage your own progress and will fail. Even if you win, it will be a short-term win. Go back to your vision for yourself and make sure you love that person you want to become.

2. Your approach did not work

What if the vision we have for ourselves is the deepest desire we have at heart and thinking about it lights our heart and brings deep joy into our lives? Then we are in luck! What you consider failure is actually a message to you that your approach, strategy and the way you were going about reaching your goal did not work. Your best friend in this case is self-reflection. Do what you need to do to relax your mind and body. Get away for a few days, meditate, practice deep breathing exercises and write down why you think your approach to accomplish your goal did not work. Be as honest as you can with yourself.

A moment of failure contains big growth opportunities, but if you do not learn what they are, the mistakes and your experiences will repeat again and again until you get the message. If you learn this, you will open magical doors to your next level! Take advantage of these moments of "failure" and do not distract yourself or keep yourself busy with things that don't matter. Take the time and learn the lesson, adjust your approach and try again!

3. The environment in which you planted your idea was not the right environment

   For an idea to take root and sprout, you need to have a supportive environment. If the wind keeps blowing hard and there is no water or nourishment in the soil, and not enough sunshine, then the seed cannot grow. You need to clear your environment from negativity and from people or things that don't support your vision and create an environment that supports your dreams. This means associating with positive people, getting help from those who are in alignment with your goals and also clearing your own internal environment; your mind and body.

A mind that lives in the past or is excessively worried about the future does not have the capacity to create, and creation happens in the now! So if this is the case for your continuous failure, clear your environment. This book offers many practical ways to help you do just that.

4. Limiting beliefs

So what if your desires truly are your deepest desires, your environment supports them, your approach to manifesting your vision is practical and in agreement with your mentor's, but still you are unable to accomplish your goals? Then it is likely that your limiting beliefs deep inside are stopping you. Do you feel scared to go after your desire and be bold about it, are you worried about failing or what others will think of you? Do you have some sort of anxiety deep inside that stops you no matter what you do, sabotages you and limits your progress? Do you think to yourself, *I don't deserve it, who am I to be successful and happy,* etc.? These are your limiting beliefs.

Be honest with yourself, and if this is the case, you are blocking your own way and making it impossible to manifest what you want. STEP 6 is all about removing these internal blockers and I encourage you to go back to this step and do the deep work. It can take you some time but I can assure you that these internal deep blockers will go away and you will see the light at the end of the tunnel. Do the work and see the magic of life! What will come to your life will take your breath away!

Utilize your superpower

Have you noticed most of the exercises in this book have been about using the power of your imagination? Imagination is an extremely powerful tool that we humans have access to. Use it properly and you can create the life of your dreams, but use it inappropriately and it will take you to dark places you don't want to go. The combination of the power of "deciding" and the magic of "imagination" are superpowers that I have seen wise and successful people use properly and, as a result, they are living a fantastic life that so many of us think is impossible for us to have. If I were going to consolidate into one sentence how to achieve your most desired life, it would be:

> Decide what kind of life you truly want, use the power of your imagination and start becoming the person that matches your vision... beginning today!

Set daily intentions

When you know who you are becoming and your eyes are set on your vision, you become a person of intention. From the moment you wake up until you go to sleep, you are living and breathing the person of your vision. You are shaping yourself with intention. This means that you set clear intentions about how you want to feel, how you want others to interact with you and you go into every interaction of your life with intention. Remember that our days are a miniature of our entire life, so how we live our life on a daily basis becomes how we live our lives overall. Do you feel you are successful, happy, moving toward your vision with intention? Then your day has been a success. Did you enjoy part of the day doing what aligns with your vision? Keep doing the best you can each day, and one day you will realize that you are living your desired life!

Absolutely take risks

If you keep doing what you have always done, you are not actually creating your life; you are playing the same record over and over. I encourage you to take new steps toward your goals every day, baby steps that are new to you and you haven't taken before, and think to yourself, *what is the worst that can happen?* If it is something that you can recover from if it doesn't work out, and will allow you to learn, grow and try new doors, then absolutely take risks. Believe in your ability to recover from failure, reflect, learn the lessons from it and move on to your next chapter.

I want you to be bold. You live life once, and unless you try new doors, you will not live a full life. So be bold, be grateful for what you have and be nice to yourself and everyone else as you explore the possibilities to create a life you love. Remember that you are the co-creator of your life! So help the universe help you!

Connect to yourself every morning

Every morning, before you engage with the world and become busy with daily tasks, school, parenting and anything else that needs your attention, you need time to connect with your vision. Look at your vision board with excitement and feel joyful, set daily intentions of how today will get you closer to your goals. Never overwhelm yourself with too much work, too many items to do and too many things to take care of. You will exhaust yourself and you will actually move further away from your desired life.

Remember, easy does it. If you have to push for something too hard, it is not meant for you. I would reserve pushing hard for short sprints that will help you finish up something when you are almost there - the last push you need to grow to the next level toward the life you want.

This kind of working hard, reserved for occasional times, brings much joy and satisfaction. The process is like building a boat. You do the daily work of cutting the wood pieces, putting them together and following the plan you have for the boat while keeping alive in your mind the final vision of enjoying the boat in the water. When the boat is almost done, you push yourself and do it naturally because you can envision yourself riding in the boat and enjoying it. Your heart is excited, you are happy, you are in the flow and in the moment and you jump into your boat and smile. You did it! You are riding in the boat that had once been only a dream and there is nothing like that in the world. The joy is real and you feel it deep in your heart and in every cell of your body. This is when pushing hard makes sense.

Celebrate small wins

Having a long-term, 3-5 year life vision is very healthy for our souls, minds and bodies. It keeps us motivated, engaged and purposeful. Remember to celebrate small wins and keep yourself motivated and engaged. It is your job to stay on the path and the way to do this is by celebrating small wins, even if the win one day is to simply get out of bed. Do what you can every day; one step at a time, one tiny improvement a day, one small step toward progress is big when done consistently. Don't worry about not making enough progress. Keep going with patience, keeping your eyes on your goal. If you take care of the process, the process will take care of the results.

FINAL WORDS

The world belongs to dreamers; people who show up in the world with clear intentions and know where they are going. When you don't have intentions, you are lost, you will go where the wind blows, you will be distracted by shiny objects that bring you deep sadness in the end, and you will be the puppet of negative people and narcissists who manipulate people with no dreams so that they can achieve their own. The material in this book is based on my life experiences and from the observations I've made of how successful people live and interact with the world. I have done extensive research so that I, my daughters and you can all use it to create a life of art and passion, and enjoy life as it was meant to be enjoyed. Remember that everyone's path is unique to them, so never compare your journey to others and confidently march toward your own destination.

I wish you peace, joy, boldness and adventure in your unique life's journey and I hope that someday you will share your learnings with the world!

Made in the USA
Middletown, DE
14 October 2021